Recognize, Respond, Report

Preventing and Addressing
Bullying of Students with Special Needs

by

Lori Ernsperger, Ph.D., BCBA-D
Henderson, Nevada

·P·A·U·L·H·
BROOKES
PUBLISHING CO ®

Baltimore • London • Sydney

Paul H. Brookes Publishing Co.
Post Office Box 10624
Baltimore, Maryland 21285–0624

www.brookespublishing.com

Copyright © 2016 by Paul H. Brookes Publishing Co., Inc.
All rights reserved.

"Paul H. Brookes Publishing Co." is a registered
trademark of Paul H. Brookes Publishing Co., Inc.

Typeset by Scribe Inc., Philadelphia, Pennsylvania.
Manufactured in the United States of America by
Sheridan Books, Chelsea, Michigan.

The individuals described in this book are composites or real people whose situations are masked and are based on the authors' experiences. In all instances, names and identifying details have been changed to protect confidentiality.

List on pp. 54–56 adapted by permission from Epstein, J.L. (2009). *School, family, and community partnerships: Your handbook for action, 3rd edition.* Thousand Oaks, CA: Corwin Press.

Library of Congress Cataloging-in-Publication Data

The Library of Congress has cataloged the print edition as follows:

Ernsperger, Lori.

    Recognize, respond, report : preventing and addressing bullying of students with special needs / by Lori Ernsperger, Ph.D., BCBA-D Autism and Behavioral Consulting, Henderson,.
        pages   cm
    Includes bibliographical references and index.
    ISBN 978-1-59857-907-9 (pbk.)—ISBN 978-1-68125-020-5 (epub)—ISBN 978-1-68125-018-2 (kindle)—ISBN 978-1-68125-021-2 (pdf)
      1. Bullying in schools—United States—Prevention.   2. Children with disabilities—Abuse of—United States.

LB3013.32.E76 2016

371.7'82—dc23   2015020050

British Library Cataloguing in Publication data are available from the British Library.

2019   2018   2017   2016   2015

10   9   8   7   6   5   4   3   2   1

Recognize, Respond, Report

Contents

About the Appendixes

Purchasers of this book have permission to photocopy the blank forms and handouts in Appendix A–F for educational use. Printable versions of these appendixes are available for download online. Please visit www.brookespublishing.com/ernsperger/materials to access these materials.

About the Author

Dr. Lori Ernsperger is an international speaker, author, and Board Certified Behavior Analyst (BCBA-D) from Henderson, Nevada, where she is the executive director of Behavioral Training Resource Center, LLC. Dr. Ernsperger received her doctorate in special education from Indiana University. She has more than 30 years of experience working in the public schools as a classroom teacher, administrator, and education consultant. Dr. Ernsperger currently provides professional development to school district personnel with a focus on bridging the gap between research and everyday practice in the classroom. Dr. Ernsperger is the author of *Keys to Success for Teaching Students with Autism, Just Take a Bite: Easy Effective Answers to Food Aversions and Eating Challenges,* and *Girls under the Umbrella of Autism Spectrum Disorders.*

Address correspondence regarding the contents of this book to drlori@cox.net.

Acknowledgments

I would like to express my sincere gratitude to the thousands of teachers and other school personnel who have willingly shared their expertise and real-life experiences in creating safe and positive school environments for all students. It is my hope to effectively pass along this sage advice. Thanks to my husband and family for supporting my numerous and sometimes wild ideas. They have allowed me to follow my passion. A special thanks to Rebecca Lazo at Paul H. Brookes Publishing Co. for your support and dedication to this project. Most important, thank you to every student and teacher who has the strength to *end the silence of others* and create a school where every child is welcomed and respected for their individuality.

Foreword

For too long, the issue of bullying among American children and adolescents with special needs has been neglected in the bullying literature. As an illustration, there are over 4,000 peer-reviewed articles on the topic of bullying, yet only 108 of these are focused on bullying among students with special needs. We are therefore a long way from a complete understanding of bullying among students with special needs and even further from instituting large-scale prevention and intervention school programs to reduce bullying among these students. While much more research has to be conducted in this area, it is time for us to educate parents, teachers, and school administrators about what we do know about bullying among students with special needs and how we can work together to address this problem. This book by Dr. Lori Ernsperger does just that.

Here, Dr. Ernsperger covers a wide range of important topics, including definitions, prevalence, and outcomes associated with bullying among students with special needs; comprehensive multitiered interventions; and specific strategies for responding to bullying. In Chapters 1 and 2, the author provides the reader with several national comprehensive definitions of bullying, emphasizing how it can manifest itself in different forms but also how it differs from normal conflict. The author distinguishes bullying from harassment and makes it very clear how schools are responsible for protecting students with special needs from bullying. She refers to the October 2013 letter from the Office for Civil Rights, which issued guidance to all school districts in the form of a Dear Colleague Letter (DCL). Although these DCLs are very informative, they are rarely seen by teachers, parents, or in many cases, school administrators. I know this because in the hundreds of talks and workshops that I do across the country, I ask audience members how many have seen these letters. In an audience of three hundred, usually five individuals will raise their hands. Thus I was thrilled to see that Dr. Ernsperger quotes the 2013 DCL in Chapter 2: "It is intolerable for teachers and school staff to be party to school bullying and disability harassment or observers to school bullying."

In order to help children who are being bullied or bullying others, it is important to understand the serious impact that bullying has on all youth involved. The short- and long-term adverse effects of bullying are described in Chapter 3, and the author explains how victims of bullying report negative consequences, including mental health symptoms and academic problems. Much has been discussed about the link between being chronically bullied and suicide ideation and behaviors. In Chapter 1, the author summarizes the association between bullying and suicidal behaviors by stating that "bullying behavior and suicide behavior are related, but not all children who are victims of bullying engage in suicidal thoughts or behaviors. There are other risk factors that may contribute to the possibility that a young person will engage in suicide-related behaviors. Other risk factors that may contribute to suicide ideation include mental health factors, environmental influences, and parenting styles." While there is not a causal link (meaning bully victimization does not cause suicide), bullying can exacerbate the risk among youth who are dealing with challenging mental health issues and/or peer rejection. As such, the author frames bullying as a form of trauma and introduces the reader to *trauma informed care*, a term that you rarely see in bullying prevention and/or intervention literature.

The author doesn't just point to the impact of bullying on individual youth but does something that many books on bullying simply don't do: she considers the impact of bullying on parents and school safety issues in general. Parents often feel isolated and helpless when they are trying to get schools to address bullying among their children. Too often, parental concerns around bullying, especially those of parents of students with special needs, are dismissed, and sometimes families and youth are blamed for the victimization. Schools need to be more responsive to parents when bullying is occurring, but schools also have the legal and ethical obligation to put prevention into place to reduce bullying. To that end, the remainder of this book includes concrete guidance on how to reduce bullying and victimization.

Human behavior is best explained through a social-ecological perspective, where there are multiple systems or structures (e.g., individual, family, schools, classrooms) interacting to drive behavior and social development. Effective interventions to reduce behaviors like bullying need to target all these systems. When I see the nine components of effective bullying prevention provided by the author, I see that she is arguing for a social-ecological framework. That is, an intervention to address bullying among students with special needs must target both risk and protective factors at each level of the social ecology, including individuals, classrooms, schools, families, and communities. Bronfenbrenner (1977) introduced the ecology of human development model, where youth are situated in systems that have direct, indirect, and dynamic influences on development and behavior. In the area of bullying, this model has often been called a social-ecological model and focuses on understanding how individual characteristics of children interact with environmental contexts or systems to promote personal safety (Espelage, 2014). The author describes how a multitiered approach should be adopted to prevent bullying. She then provides great detail about how to intervene with individual youth involved in the bully–victim dynamic, how to create safe and supportive classrooms, how to foster a positive school climate, and how to address bullying through social-emotional learning curricula.

Indeed, when school staff and teachers perceive a poor school climate, students report greater rates of bullying and victimization (Espelage, Polanin, & Low, 2014). Thus, increasingly, bullying prevention is being seen as involving a school climate improvement process that involves all stakeholders. This book provides excellent guidance for schools to implement a school climate improvement plan and ways to attend to larger school safety issues. Several chapters address staff training, teacher training, and engaging youth in the process of school improvement. The author also provides concrete ways in which parents and caregivers can be connected to the prevention of bullying among special needs youth. Also, I truly appreciated the attention given to social-emotional learning approaches to bullying prevention. We do know that when social-emotional learning programs are implemented with fidelity, there is less disruptive behaviors, less bullying, and better learning in classrooms (Durlak, Weissberg, Dymnicki, Taylor, & Schellinger, 2011; Espelage, Rose, & Polanin, 2015). As noted by the author, these programs are only effective when they are implemented with fidelity and when they fit into a multitiered program that focuses on sustainability.

Effective bullying prevention and intervention involves comprehensive programming that targets all levels of the social ecology through a multitiered framework like the one described in this book. However, it can be challenging to understand how to integrate all these ways of recognizing, responding to, and reporting bullying, especially among students with special needs. Now there is definitive guidance for schools with this book. From my perspective, this is a unique book on bullying because it focuses on students with special needs but also provides clear, concrete, and evidence-based strategies. Thus, this is a must-read book for school administrators, interventionists, teachers, parents, and youth leaders who are driving their school antibullying campaigns.

Dorothy Espelage, Ph.D.
Edward William Gutgsell & Jane Marr Gutgsell Endowed Professor
Hardie Professor of Education
Department of Educational Psychology
University of Illinois, Champaign

Preface

The Silence of Others

There are a variety of reasons why people are passionate about bullying prevention in schools. Some school professionals have had personal experiences that have driven them to become vocal advocates for at-risk populations. Other educators focus on creating a positive school climate, and still others may have been assigned job responsibilities within the school to address school safety and harassment. Whatever the reasons for the upsurge of national attention by educators, bullying prevention in schools has become an important safety issue across the globe. For me personally, the reason for writing this book and sharing my message is because of Michelle. I met Michelle several years ago while writing another book, *Girls under the Umbrella of Autism Spectrum Disorders*. I interviewed Michelle when she was in her early 20s, and she was eager to share her life story about growing up in the Midwest with mild autism spectrum disorder (ASD). Michelle spoke lovingly of her siblings and her interest in ballroom dancing. The conversation was insightful and portrayed a young woman with many positive life experiences, but the mood and tone of the conversation changed dramatically when the topic switched to her school years after the family moved to the West Coast when she was 12. Michelle shared the horrific stories of bullying that occurred for several years at her new school. She was the target of social exclusion, verbal assaults, and constant rumors through no fault of her own. Although Michelle was able to recount in detail some terrible personal experiences that might cause one to feel singled out, she had come to understand that she was not the only target for bullying in her school. She recognized that bullying often occurs during middle school, and it was not something she could control. According to Michelle, "I saw lots of other kids teased and pushed around. It wasn't just me, and I forgive the bullies. However, what I cannot forgive is the *silence of others*." I asked Michelle to explain what she meant by the *silence of others*. She said that she made many attempts to report this daily bullying to teachers, but they simply told her not to worry about it and just ignore it. She also had the courage to meet with the principal to share her story, and he said he "would look into it." Even her parents were unable to make a difference and stop the bullying. The lack of action and intervention by all of the adults and other students is what Michele referred to as the *silence of others,* and it is something that she is unable to forgive and forget.

After our interview, I sat down to rewrite my notes and summarize the insightful information shared with me. I continued to ponder her statement about the *silence of others,* and I realized she was talking about *me.* I had worked with individuals with disabilities for almost 30 years, starting as a Special Olympics volunteer in high school, then as a special education teacher, behavior specialist, administrator, college professor, and ASD consultant. Not once in all those years had I addressed the issue of bullying and individuals with disabilities. I even held a job with the Indiana Department of Education that oversaw special education services for the entire state and never was there a discussion of disability-based harassment. I have traveled extensively both in the United States and internationally, speaking to large groups of school personnel for professional development, and yet I had never included evidence-based interventions for bullying prevention in my presentation. I had to face reality: *I, too, had remained silent for years.* That is when I made a promise to Michelle to increase awareness and disseminate positive and proactive educational interventions to stop bullying in schools. As a part of my promise, I came up with the framework of *Recognize, Respond, Report (3 Rs),* which details practical and powerful measures for bullying prevention of students with disabilities. My book focuses on each of the 3 Rs in three distinct parts, helping school personnel and parents effectively work together to address the issue of bullying and its effects on student well-being and end the *silence of others.*

OVERVIEW OF THE BOOK

Part I: Recognize Bullying and Disability-Based Harassment in Schools

- Chapter 1 covers the startling prevalence rates of bullying in schools and the current statistics for disability-based harassment. This chapter describes the reasons why students with disabilities are vulnerable to bullying. In addition, Chapter 1 defines bullying and provides keywords and criteria for understanding the definition of harassment.

- Chapter 2 contains a description of the different types of bullying and explains the bully–victim dynamic. This chapter also reveals the difficult and often undisclosed issue of staff mistreatment of students and recommends the need for highly effective staff training to improve overall school climate.

- Chapter 3 delves into the serious mental health effects of bullying and harassment. This chapter examines the impact of bullying, such as increased absenteeism and lower academic achievement. In addition, Chapter 3 explores bullying within larger school safety issues and the need to avoid zero tolerance policies as disciplinary measures for bullying in schools.

Part II: Respond to Bullying and Disability-Based Harassment in Schools

- Chapter 4 presents the core components for an effective comprehensive bullying prevention program. The chapter highlights the need for a multitiered response to bullying and harassment: district- and schoolwide, classroom-level, and individualized targeted interventions. Chapter 4 also provides detailed recommendations for schoolwide activities, such as how to create a school safety team, with free resources to monitor sustained practices.

- Chapter 5 focuses on classroom-level interventions that can be easily implemented across grade levels. Simple lessons for teaching social-emotional learning and bullying awareness are provided with suggestions for embedding activities within the existing curriculum.

- Chapter 6 addresses the distinct needs of students with disabilities who are vulnerable to bullying. Bystander education programs are reviewed with resources for creating peer mentoring programs. Chapter 6 also contains specific interventions for addressing students with disabilities who exhibit bullying behaviors as well as possible graduated consequences.

Part III: Report Bullying and Disability-Based Harassment in Schools

- Chapter 7 promotes data-based decision making at all levels of school interventions. Recommendations are given for creating student surveys and organizing focus groups for data collection. Chapter 7 focuses on results-driven accountability at all levels.

- Chapter 8 presents the essential features for developing and distributing a school bullying report form. This chapter outlines specific action steps for investigating bullying and determining disability-based harassment. Chapter 8 lists possible corrective measures for schools to adopt if a harassment violation has been determined.

- Chapter 9 walks the reader through practical techniques for analyzing and visually organizing the data for the purposes of school improvement planning. Chapter 9 underscores the need to adopt strict adherence to implementation fidelity and sustained practices in order to achieve long-term positive outcomes and safe schools.

RESOURCES AND SPECIAL FEATURES

Additional resources and special features are provided throughout this book. You will see several icons that direct you to more information on the topic or free materials available to download. In addition, student quotes have been interspersed throughout the text in order to emphasize the importance of preventing and responding to bullying.

Online resources: The World Wide Web icon directs you to online resources to further your knowledge on the topic and gain additional information that can be utilized in schools.

Downloadable toolkits and manuals: The download icon indicates free materials available for school personnel to download. These free toolkits and materials are often ready to use in the classroom.

Student quotes: The speech bubble icon provides real-life responses from middle and high school students. A group of 250 students were asked to respond to a variety of fictional "Dear Abby" letters and give their advice for dealing with bullying in schools. The student quotes are honest and heartfelt responses to their fellow students.

Recognize

Roses are red,

Violets are blue,

Just be who you are,

And people will soon love you.

Prevalence and Definition of Bullying and Disability-Based Harassment

Bullying was once a silent epidemic endured by millions of children daily. The attitude "kids will be kids" was considered just a part of normal childhood development. Most school professionals do not recognize the severe implications of bullying, its long-term impact on childhood victims, and its overall negative impact on the school environment and student achievement. Today, bullying in schools is being recognized as an international problem and public health concern. Recognizing the startling international and national statistics on bullying in schools is the first step in developing a comprehensive bullying and disability-based harassment prevention program:

- The U.S. Department of Education estimates that 28% of all middle school and high school students are bullied in school (Robers et al., 2012).

- The World Health Organization reported that in a study of more than 15,000 students, 29.9% reported moderate or frequent involvement in bullying (Nansel et al., 2001).

- The Centers for Disease Control and Prevention indicate that approximately 20% of students report being bullied across various grade levels (Eaton et al., 2011).

- The National Crime Victimization Survey (2011) states that 27% of boys reported being bullied, whereas 30% of girls reported being bullied, dispelling the myth that there are differences between the prevalence rates for girls and boys.

- The National Center for Education Statistics' "Indicators of School Crime and Safety" (2008) indicates that 24% of elementary and secondary students are bullied weekly, with 7% of students bullied every day.

Taken in its totality, bullying is a severe and significant problem facing millions of children. Although there is some variability in the total percentage of the prevalence of bullying due to definition standards and measurement tools, it is clear that bullying affects millions of students in the United States annually.

 I have been bullied since the 4th grade. I am short and skinny. I am alone and it makes me cry. I know there are bullies in every school, and I am trying to make friends too. Good luck.

In addition to the high rates of bullying for typically developing students, students with special needs are bullied at twice the rate of their peers. According to several national and state surveys and assessment outcomes, students with disabilities are at a greater risk for bullying and harassment:

- Ability Path (2011) reports that 60% of students with disabilities are bullied in schools.

- The Interactive Autism Network (IAN, 2012) reported that 63% of students with autism spectrum disorders (ASDs) were bullied in schools.

- *Youth Voice Project* (Davis & Nixon, 2014) reports that students with physical disabilities were 1.94 times more likely to be bullied in schools and students receiving special education were 1.66 times more likely to be bullied.

- The U.S. Department of Education reports children with learning disabilities, epilepsy, and other special needs are at a greater risk of being bullied and harassed (U.S. Department of Education, n.d.).

Bullying is increasingly disproportional when involving students with disabilities (Young, Ne'eman, & Gelser, 2011). Students with physical disabilities are at a greater risk for being targets of bullying (Rose, Swearer, & Espelage, 2012). Sixty-nine percent of students who stutter report that bullying occurs very frequently (Langevin, Bortnick, Hammer, & Wiebe, 1998). Students taking medication in school for attention-deficit/hyperactivity disorder (ADHD) face two to three times more bullying in schools per month than typical peers (Unnever & Cornell, 2003). According to Davis and Nixon's *Youth Voice Project* (2014), "Students who are members of groups who are not valued by the school community are more likely to be mistreated and ostracized socially," which leads to social exclusion. Students with disabilities are unfortunately often isolated and not included as part of the school environment. In addition to students with more obvious visible and recognized disabilities, students with other health needs are also more likely to be bullied in schools. For example, students with a chronic illness such as asthma or diabetes report higher rates of bullying (Sentenac et al., 2012). These high rates of bullying and disability-based harassment have finally garnered the attention of school professionals, state educational agencies, and the federal government as a public health concern (Hamburger, Basile, & Vivolo, 2011), which warrants effective, comprehensive programming.

 Tell the principal about the boys on the bus. You need to get a strict bus driver. Once you get a new bus driver, sit in the front and when kids call you names, tell the bus driver. Even if the kids call you snitch afterward, that just gives you more of a reason to stand up to them.

PREVALENCE AND DEFINITION OF BULLYING

Due to the severe and often long-term negative impact of and public health concerns about bullying and harassment, it is important for federal, state, and local educational leaders to adopt a uniform definition of bullying. Definitions of bullying can vary from state to state and school to school, which is a factor contributing to the variability of prevalence rates. The federal government has not adopted a universal definition for bullying in schools. To this end, the Centers for Disease Control and Prevention (CDC, 2014) selected an expert panel of researchers and practitioners to create a definition of bullying for use by schools and other public health agencies for further research on evidence-based interventions and assessment tools. The CDC and U.S. Department of Education (2014) released the following definition of bullying:

> Bullying is any unwanted aggressive behavior(s) by another youth or group of youths who are not siblings or current dating partners that involves an observed or perceived power imbalance and repeated multiple times or is highly likely to be repeated. Bullying may inflict harm or distress on the targeted youth including physical, psychological, social, or educational harm. (p. 7)

There are other national organizations that have also developed position statements that include a definition of bullying. For example, the National Education Association (NEA) has written a slightly different definition of bullying:

> Bullying is systematically and chronically inflicting physical hurt and/or psychological distress on another. Bullying can be physical, verbal or social. Bullying is not just child's play, but a frightening experience many students face every day. Bullying involves a real or perceived power imbalance between the one who bullies and their target. (NEA, n.d.)

Dan Olweus is a pioneer in the field of school safety and bullying prevention in schools. His work and research have been around for more than two decades and are cited as seminal research in the field of bullying. His groundbreaking book, *Bullying at School* (1993), was written after the tragic suicides of three young boys in Norway in 1983 caused the adoption of new anti-bullying laws. The Olweus Bullying Prevention Program (OBPP) defines bullying as when "someone repeatedly and on purpose says or does mean or hurtful things to another person who has a hard time defending himself or herself" (Olweus, 1993). The OBPP program has expanded internationally and is a widely used multitiered program that has demonstrated significant positive results in decreasing bullying in schools (Farrington & Ttofi, 2010). There are keywords and common terms for defining bullying (Table 1.1).

Most definitions of bullying include a perceived imbalance of power. This can be due to appearance, body size, personality characteristics, degree of masculinity or femininity, socioeconomic status, or academic performance in school. Power imbalance can be subjective in nature and may require further explanation to students and staff by demonstrating exemplars of differing characteristics that create a power imbalance—for example, the outgoing boisterous captain of the football team versus the shy introvert computer club president or students from an influential geographical area of town versus students who live in impoverished neighborhoods.

 I can relate because in 8th grade I was a new kid and I didn't know anyone. I got bullied because I was shy and dressed different from anyone. I finally got out of it in high school because I starting talking more and gained confidence. I believe in you. If they say something to you that is mean, just say, "Does it look like I care?"

In addition to the common terms and language utilized for defining bullying, some state and local definitions of bullying include an additional criteria that bullying is an *intentional, deliberate,* or *willful* act, which is a threshold much more challenging for school officials to investigate. As one might imagine, when confronted by an adult, it would not be uncommon for a student who exhibited a bullying act to quickly state, "I didn't mean it" or "I was just messing with them," thus minimizing the action or intent. Determining a person's intention is

Table 1.1.   Common terms and keywords for defining bullying

- Repeated actions
- Harmful to the victim
- Unwelcome behavior
- Inflicted on someone with less power or perceived power differences or dominance

subjective for school professionals who may be investigating an incident of bullying. According to the Dear Colleague Letter (DCL) from the U.S. Department of Education, Office of Civil Rights (OCR, 2010), "Harassment does not have to include *intent* to harm" (p. 2).

In addition, Dr. Jorge Srabstein, Medical Director of the Clinic for Health Problems Related to Bullying, states that "intentionality may not be required criteria when considering bullying" (Srabstein, 2014). Regardless of the intent, the hostile action exhibited by a student or group of students is unwelcome conduct based on the perception of the victim. The severity or negative impact of bullying or disability-based harassment is not solely judged by whether the act was intentional or not. Dr. Srabstein (2014) goes on to say, "Bullying is in the eyes of the beholder." When investigating a bullying incident to determine disability-based harassment, the question is not whether the student "intended" to create a hostile environment. The incident is examined through the perspective of the victim or more likely a student with a disability. As will be discussed in Chapter 4, it is imperative that school professionals develop a uniform definition of bullying that includes the standard criteria for harassment and is disseminated to all school staff, students, and parents.

What Is a Dear Colleague Letter?

Dear Colleague Letters (DCLs) are official correspondence and nonregulatory guidance letters from the U.S. Department of Education to school districts, charter school operators, and school personnel for implementing federal laws and civil rights requirements. DCLs are available to members of the public (parents, students, and community stakeholders), with information about their rights and examples to assist these groups in meeting their legal obligations. They are not intended to set forth any new laws or require specific actions by any state, school, or school district, but schools should carefully consider adopting these policies and interventions as best practice standards when addressing bullying prevention and ending disability-based harassment.

Bullying versus Normal Childhood Conflict

When recognizing and defining bullying in schools, educators must often distinguish between typical childhood behaviors and bullying. Not all peer-to-peer teasing or aggression is bullying, and school professionals should be careful when defining bullying for staff and students in an attempt to distinguish between observable behaviors. According to Barbara Coloroso (2008), "teasing is a fun thing to do with friends and is a playful part of childhood development" (p. 32). Childhood conflict is a normal part of the social environment in a school setting. Children that are of equal status and friends will have normal peer

Table 1.2.   Examples of normal childhood conflict versus bullying

A group of longtime friends poke fun at each other in a lighthearted manner in the cafeteria. One student burps in the other student's face. The peer then sticks his finger in the student's mashed potatoes. Both students have an equal friendship, and they leave the cafeteria together while laughing.	A student sitting alone in the cafeteria is approached by an older student who calls him "retarded and gay" and then pours his milk on his tray. Other students laugh at him, and the perpetrator walks away leaving the student sitting alone.
Two girls with equal power and status have an argument, insult each other, and scream they will never speak again. When confronted by an adult, they immediately have remorse for their actions and end the disagreement.	Two girls have what appears to be a disagreement that has been ongoing in the classroom for weeks. The dominant girl says, "You are a skank." When an adult intervenes, the dominant girl shifts blames and has no remorse for her actions.

conflict and may even exhibit rude or mean behaviors. It is important to recognize that not all childhood struggles constitute bullying. Minor acts of childhood struggles are a normal part of development and must be differentiated from harmful acts of aggression toward students at risk (Limber & Snyder, 2006). The written school definition of bullying, for both staff and students, may include examples or different representations of normal childhood conflict versus bullying to ensure consistent understanding between these concepts. Teachers and school leaders should provide age-appropriate concrete examples of behaviors that are considered part of bullying (e.g., repeated name calling and pushing of a younger student) and differentiate examples of normal childhood conflict (e.g., like poking fun at a friend). A school district's operational definition of bullying should provide degrees, characteristics, and exemplars of normal peer conflict and examples of bullying for comparison (Table 1.2).

Well here is my advice because I go through the same thing and it is hard, but when people tell me I'm ugly, I just say, "Before you judge me, make sure you are perfect." Don't let them bother you, and that makes them mad. I hope you can take my advice and keep your head up.

Disability-Based Harassment

According to research from a variety of international and national disability organizations and governmental agencies, students with disabilities are vulnerable and at greater risk for being bullied in schools, which may rise to the level of disability-based harassment. School personnel must first recognize and understand that students with disabilities have additional legal protections to guard against hostile environments, such as bullying in school. Students with disabilities have a greater protection from bullying and disability harassment under three federal laws:

1. Section 504 of the Rehabilitation Act of 1973 (PL 93-112) is an antidiscrimination law designed to protect the rights of individuals with disabilities in programs and activities that receive federal financial assistance from the U.S. Department of Education.

2. Title II of the Americans with Disabilities Act of 2008 (PL 110-325) is an antidiscrimination law that extends the prohibition to the full range of state and local government services, programs, and activities (including public schools).

3. The Individuals with Disabilities Education Improvement Act (IDEA) of 2004 (PL 108-446) is a federal statute that funds special education programs and requires a school district to provide a free appropriate public education (FAPE) to students with disabilities in the least restrictive environment (LRE).

The federal government has a long history of creating and implementing strict laws to protect individuals with disabilities from harassment. From 1973 to the present day, a series of federal laws have been enacted and reauthorized explicitly to protect individuals with disabilities from any form of discrimination, which includes harassment, in schools. In order for a student to make a claim of disability harassment, they must first be found eligible or qualify for services under the federal regulations of the Individuals with Disabilities Education Act (IDEA) or Section 504 of the Rehabilitation Act of 1973. A student is found eligible for special education and related services for a disability under IDEA after an individualized educational evaluation determines if the student meets the criteria within the 13 specific disability categories: "In order to fully meet the definition (and eligibility for special education and related services) as a 'child with a disability,' a child's educational performance must be adversely affected due to a disability" (IDEA, 2004; Table 1.3).

For more information on specific disability categories, go to Center for Parent Information and Resources web site:

 http://www.parentcenterhub.org/repository/categories

Table 1.3.   Individuals with Disabilities Education Act (IDEA) disability categories

Autism	Multiple disabilities	Deaf blindness	Deafness
	Emotional disturbance	Hearing impairment	Orthopedic impairment
Other health impairment	Specific learning disability	Speech language impairment	
Intellectual disability	Traumatic brain injury	Visual impairment including blindness	

A student may also claim disability-based harassment if they qualify under Section 504, which defines an individual with a disability as "any person who: (i) has a mental or physical impairment that substantially limits one or more major life activity; (ii) has a record of such an impairment; or (iii) is regarded as having such an impairment" (34 C.F.R. §104.3[j][I]). Students who qualify under Section 504 and demonstrate an impairment that limits a major life activity (e.g., walking, learning, reading, thinking) can range from those with severe allergies, medical conditions such as diabetes, ADHD, or other issues that limit their school activity. Students who qualify as having a disability under Section 504 have a written 504 Plan that includes supports and accommodations to their educational program. For more information on Section 504 and protecting students with disabilities, go to the U.S. Department of Education web site:

http://www2.ed.gov/about/offices/list/ocr/504faq.html

Students who qualify as having a disability under IDEA automatically receive protections from discrimination, such as harassment, under Section 504 and Title II. Although the qualifications and standards for students under IDEA are much more stringent with specific eligibility criteria, students who qualify under Section 504 are awarded the same rights of protection from disability-based harassment (OCR, 2010, 2014). Section 504 protects individuals with disabilities, including IDEA-eligible students, from discrimination and ensures that children with disabilities have equal access to an education. Although there are major differences in the qualifications under these two federal laws, it is important for school personnel to understand that both groups of students are protected from discrimination, which includes bullying and disability-based harassment (OCR, 2010, 2014).

Definition of *Students with Disabilities*

For the purpose of this book, the term *students with disabilities* will include students found eligible for special education aids and services under both IDEA and Section 504.

In addition to these federal antidiscrimination laws and funding statutes, the U.S. Department of Education has provided technical assistance and guidance to school districts regarding bullying and disability-based harassment with four important DCLs. Beginning with the first DCL on July 25, 2000, the Office for Civil Rights (OCR) has provided clear guidance for the compliance with the federal laws to protect individuals with disabilities as well as other protected classes such as race, color, gender, religion, and sexual orientation. The OCR, under direction from the Department of Education, has clarified the relationship among bullying, harassment, and the legal requirements for school district personnel to investigate and prevent future incidents. According to the OCR (2000),

> Disability harassment can have a profound impact on students, raise safety concerns, and erode efforts to ensure that students with disabilities have equal access to the myriad benefits that an education offers. Indeed, harassment can seriously interfere with the ability of students with disabilities to receive the education critical to their advancement. When disability harassment limits or denies a student's ability to participate in or benefit from an educational institution's programs or activities, the institution must respond effectively. Where the institution learns that disability harassment may have occurred, the institution must investigate the incident(s) promptly and respond appropriately. (p. 1)

The OCR reminds schools that the failure to recognize disability-based harassment may be a violation of students' civil rights. In a follow-up letter dated October 26, 2010, the OCR recognized that state and local educational agencies had expanded policies and procedures specifically to address bullying in schools, but these general school policies and procedures on bullying may not protect students from disability-based harassment. OCR explains, "By limiting its response to a specific application of its anti-bullying disciplinary policy, a school may fail to properly consider whether the student misconduct also results in discriminatory harassment" (p. 1). School district personnel must heed caution when applying a standard of bullying during an incident involving a student with a disability. For example, if an adopted school policy requires that an incident of bullying include "deliberate acts," then a violation of disability-based harassment may not be determined with this requirement of intentional acts. The school may dismiss acts that are ultimately disability-based harassment due to this additional requirement, potentially violating a student's right to a "hostile-free" educational environment.

The DCLs from the OCR are clear with regard to their expectations and guidance to all school district leaders and school professionals. In addition to the DCLs written from the OCR (2000, 2010, 2014), the Department of Education in conjunction with the Office of Special Education and Rehabilitative Services (OSERS) wrote a DCL on August 20, 2013, to clarify its position on bullying and disability-based harassment as it relates to a student's right to a free appropriate public education (FAPE). The OSERS's letter states that "bullying, for any reason cannot be tolerated in our schools . . . and students with disabilities have a right to a safe and respectful school environment" (p. 1). The letter goes on to state that "whether or not the bullying is related to the student's disability, any bullying of a student with disabilities that results in the student not receiving meaningful educational benefit constitutes a denial of a FAPE" (p. 3). The Department of Education is suggesting that bullying can seriously interfere with students with disabilities' right "to receive the education critical to their advancement" (OCR, 2000). This DCL (2013) reminds school personnel of their responsibility for addressing all incidents of bullying and potential disability-based harassment, which creates a hostile environment to a student with a disability regardless of the intentionality or label used to describe the incident (e.g., bullying, hazing, teasing). This type of repeated unwelcome behavior creates a hostile environment and interferes with the student's ability to participate in or benefit from the services, activities, or opportunities provided by the school (CDC, 2014). To watch a short video on disability-based harassment, visit StopBullying.gov:

 http://www.stopbullying.gov/videos/2014/02/civil-rights.html

It is important to clarify that bullying and harassment can overlap (CDC, 2014). School personnel may ask, when does bullying become disability harassment? The OCR does not utilize the term "bullying" but instead prohibits "harassment." In a DCL regarding *Santa Monica (CA) Unified School District, 55 IDELR 208* (OCR, 2010), OCR explains,

> Although the possible bases for action constituting "bullying" are much broader than the bases constituting harassment under federal laws enforced by OCR, because the complaint stated actions alleged to have taken against the Student because of disability, the distinction between "bullying" and harassment in this matter is *immaterial* and the complaint was investigated as one alleging harassment.

Therefore, the school's labeling of an incident as "bullying" is immaterial if the student has a disability under the protections of federal regulations. Table 1.4 provides the language and legal definitions that constitute disability-based harassment.

If the criteria listed in Table 1.4 are met, then a finding of disability-based harassment violation may be proven. Even if one of the criteria is not met, for a student who is receiving IDEA FAPE services or 504 FAPE services, the school multidisciplinary team should convene to determine whether the student's educational needs have changed.

As clear and forthright as the Department of Education and OCR have been with clarifying the rights of students with disabilities (OCR, 2000, 2010, 2013, 2014),

Table 1.4. Four-prong criteria for disability-based harassment

1. The student is an individual with a disability and receives unwelcome conduct or harassment based on his or her disability.

2. The bullying is sufficiently severe, persistent, or pervasive to create a hostile environment.

3. School officials know or reasonably should have known about the harassment.

4. The school failed to respond appropriately to end the harassment. School personnel must take immediate action to eliminate the hostile environment and prevent it from recurring and, as appropriate, remedy its effects.

Source: Adapted from U.S. Center for Parent Information and Resources. (2015). Categories of disability under IDEA. United States Department of Education, Office of Special Education Programs. Retrieved from http://www.parentcenterhub.org/repository/categories

there remains a gap in knowledge of these protections at the school level as these groundbreaking and important documents are not widely disseminated to front-line school personnel. For example, while attending a special education seminar held in a rural southern town, I informally surveyed the 87 participants of their knowledge of the DCLs: Only 3 attendees (out of 87) had any awareness of the existence of these DCLs, and just one participant understood the legal implications for school personnel. This small sample is not intended to represent the millions of teachers and staff who work in schools but may suggest an indication for the need of further professional development and widespread awareness campaigns of the federally required protections for students with disabilities.

 When I was in 3rd grade, I was pushed around because I was bigger than most of my friends. Even when I lost weight, I still got talked about. When they say things, I just say to myself, "That's not who I am anymore." Become the bigger person and just keep walking like you never heard them and stay happy. Never show you care.

The multiple and compelling technical assistance guidance letters from the Department of Education, the OCR, and the OSERS provide further evidence of the federal government's position on protecting students with disabilities in schools. The Department of Education reminds all school personnel of their important role in defining bullying and quickly investigating any claims of disability harassment and to prevent any further incidents. School leaders must recognize that educational institutions are held legally accountable to provide an educational environment that ensures equal educational opportunities for all students (OCR, 2010). Given the high rates of bullying of students with disabilities, it is critically important that all special education professionals recognize the signs of bullying, disability harassment, and their legal obligations to intervene. If schools reasonably suspect disability harassment, they must take prompt, effective steps to eliminate the hostile environment.

In addition to the federal regulations and DCL guidance from the Department of Education regarding disability-based harassment, there are additional legal ramifications for school personnel as parents pursue legal remedies for cases of bullying and harassment. There have been several due process hearings and federal court cases with regard to harassment and students' civil rights. Parents are becoming more informed of their rights and the rights of their children with disabilities as a number of state legislatures pass new laws, policies, and procedures. In 2011, a New York federal judge ruled in a precedent-setting case regarding bullying and harassment for students receiving special education services known as *T.K. v New York Department of Education* (Cyr, 2012). A 12-year-old girl with a learning disability and her parents had repeatedly complained to the principal of bullying in school. The school did not take adequate steps to investigate and prevent future bullying. The district court ruled in favor of the parents that their daughter was denied IDEA FAPE services based largely on the OCR Harassment and Bullying Guidance Letter (2010). Although the New York district court case findings cannot legally be applied at a national level to all schools, the ruling is a reminder of the strict duties of school personnel to take prompt and appropriate action when students with disabilities are bullied or harassed. School personnel who violate federal law and do not investigate and eliminate disability harassment can create potential liabilities for the school, opening themselves up for lawsuits, which are time consuming, include damages and attorney fees, and can jeopardize the students' civil rights. If school personnel are reasonably made aware of harassment toward a student with a disability, they are required by federal law to investigate and take action to end the hostile environment. Chapter 8 will review the laws and requirements for investigating disability harassment and the corrective measures that should be taken by school leaders.

Implementation Checklist

Can you . . . ?   **Yes**

Review and articulate the prevalence of bullying   ☐

Identify the impact of bullying on students with disabilities   ☐

Memorize the keywords and common language to define bullying   ☐

Differentiate between bullying and normal childhood conflict   ☐

Label the three federal laws that protect students with disabilities   ☐

Indicate the four-prong criteria for disability-based harassment   ☐

List the legal ramifications of harassment in schools   ☐

Types of Bullying

In addition to recognizing the prevalence and definition of bullying and disability-based harassment in schools and the vulnerability of students with disabilities, school professionals must also recognize the complex nature and various forms of bullying. Some forms of bullying and harassment are widespread and can be easily observed (e.g., physical aggression), whereas other forms of bullying are insidious and require careful investigation and awareness (e.g., social exclusion). Whether a student is a "child with a disability" (according to IDEA or Section 504) or a typically developing student within the general education setting, bullying can take many forms, including verbal teasing, physical aggression, and social exclusion. Table 2.1 lists the various types of bullying.

Regardless of the type of bullying or the perceived level of aggression or social exclusion, it is important for all school personnel to remember that demeaning jokes, repeated insults, or mocking someone based on race, color, gender, religion, sexual orientation, and disability is bullying that could reasonably be considered harassment if the conduct is sufficiently severe, pervasive, or persistent (OCR, 2010). School district personnel must recognize conduct such as verbal and threatening behavior based on a student's disability that limits the student from benefiting from an education program (OCR, 2010). Prejudicial remarks such as "gay," "fag," "retarded," or any other insult based on these protected classes must be recognized as harassment when they create a hostile environment. This type of harassment must be addressed within written school policy and procedures for bullying prevention. All school personnel must consistently tackle the use of discriminatory language in schools and provide direct feedback for all disrespectful behaviors. Welcoming Schools is a project from the Human Rights Campaign that offers professional tools, lesson plans aligned with the Common Core State Standards, and

Table 2.1. Types of bullying

Type of bullying	Definition and examples
Physical aggression	Most school professionals can easily identify physical acts of aggression such as hitting, punching, slapping, kicking, shoving, tripping, and pushing another student as bullying. Physical acts of bullying can also include blocking access to a classroom or school function.
Verbal bullying	Abusive teasing, intimidation, name calling, taunting, threatening, aggressive gestures, and direct intimidation are more overt and observable within the school environment.
Relational, social, emotional bullying	Relational bullying can include social exclusion, alienation, withdrawing attention, attempts to harm a student's reputation through gossip and rumor mills, and repeated rejection to social advances. Relational bullying often goes undetected and unreported by school personnel (Swearer, Espelage, & Napolitano, 2009). Relational bullying is associated more with female bullying and based on criticism of physical attributes and personal characteristics (Besag, 2006).
Destruction of property	This form of bullying involves the destruction or defacement of another's property and damage to school materials and personal property, including phones, computers, backpacks, and other devices.
Cyberbullying	Cyberbullying is bullying that takes place using electronic technology. Examples of cyberbullying include mean text messages or e-mails; rumors sent by e-mail or posted on social-networking sites; and embarrassing pictures, videos, web sites, or fake profiles.

many additional resources to assist schools in addressing diversity and avoiding gender stereotypes. Welcoming Schools offers administrators, educators, and parents materials necessary to create supportive learning environments in which all students are welcomed and respected. The Welcoming Schools program has also developed a quick and easy guide for all staff called "What Do You Say to 'That's so Gay'?" This comprehensive guide provides school staff with straightforward responses and reminders of how to effectively respond to offensive language and can be modified for other discriminatory insults such as "That's so retarded."

For more information, go to http://www.welcomingschools.org/pages/ what-do-you-say-to-thats-so-gay/

I know your situation seems hopeless, but I am here to tell you don't worry. Other kids are insecure. It is wrong that they make fun of you. However, you have to realize that everyone is uncomfortable in their own shoes. You are not alone.

CYBERBULLYING

National research and local media coverage highlight the prevalence of cyber-bullying as a growing problem in public schools and the community. According to Dr. Hinduja and Dr. Patchin from the Cyberbullying Research Center, approx-imately 25.2% of students surveyed experienced cyberbullying in their lifetimes (Hinduja & Patchin, 2015). Another report from the Youth Risk Behavior Sur-veillance Survey (Eaton et al., 2011) reported that 16% of high school students (Grades 9–12) were electronically bullied in the past year. Currently, there are no national data on cyberbullying as it directly relates to students with disabilities, but there is no denying the real threat of cyberbullying and its effects on school achievement and overall school climate.

Flag the Facebook account. One easy solution to the problem is remove yourself from the social network. Simply stay away from Facebook and Twit-ter and delete your pictures. Just delete the whole account. It is illegal to put mean stuff on Facebook.

Cyberbullying is a complicated issue for school personnel, with rapidly changing advances in technology and First Amendment rights for students. Therefore, it is not within the breadth of this book to adequately address cyber-bullying research and practical interventions for schools. It is important to remember that many of the interventions described in this book can apply to pre-venting and reducing cyberbullying in schools (e.g., awareness campaigns, youth involvement, professional development). For more information on preventing and responding to cyberbullying, the following books and web sites provide a thorough synthesis of the current literature and recommendations for educators:

Cyberbullying: Bullying in the Digital Age (Kowalski, Limber, & Agatston, 2012)

Bullying Beyond the Schoolyard (Hinduja & Patchin, 2015)

Cyberbullying Research Center (http://cyberbullying.us)

National Center for Missing and Exploited Children: Netsmartz (http://www.netsmartz.org)

BULLY–VICTIM DYNAMIC

The lines between the bully and the victim are often blurred. It is not uncom-mon for students to be a bully in some instances and the victim on other occa-sions. Research suggests that 70%–80% of students will be involved in a bullying incident at some point in their school career as a bully, victim, or bystander (Gra-ham, 2011). In a recent study of students with autism spectrum disorders (ASDs),

ASD students were identified as victims 46.3% of the time, perpetrators 14.8% of the time, and both victim and perpetrator 8.9% of the time (Sterzing, Shattuck, Narendorf, Wagner, & Cooper, 2012). A *bully* or *victim* is not a forever label, as behaviors can change dramatically from year to year. School staff should avoid the labeling of students and focus on the observable behaviors that are associated with bullying, such as name calling, pushing, or excluding peers from social activities. See StopBullying.gov for a short video for staff and students on the importance of avoiding labeling:

 http://www.stopbullying.gov/videos/2014/03/labels-dont-define-you.html

Based on past experiences and societal stereotypes, most all of us can conjure up an image of the schoolyard bully. Bullies are often stereotyped as a muscular male who lacks empathy, a loner who struggles in school, a student with conduct problems or delinquency who has a challenging homelife, or a student with low self-esteem with few friends. However, these myths are inaccurate and narrow and limit our ability to effectively address bullying in schools as we filter through a myopic lens of stereotypes. According to Dr. Susan Swearer, "There is no way to profile a bully. Almost anyone can be a bully" (2010).

In order for teachers and school personnel to better understand bullying in schools, research has been conducted to allow for some generalizations about traits or characteristics associated with bullying behaviors. For example, students who exhibit bullying behaviors are often socially adept and have a keen insight into how other people are feeling and thinking (Swearer, Espelage, & Napolitano, 2009). Bullies seek to gain admiration and positive peer influence from other students who witness incidents of bullying (Salmivalli, 2010). Bullying behaviors are maintained by positive attention from peers, the reaction of the victim, and reinforcement from the bystanders. In a recent study published by the *Journal of Youth and Adolescence* (Juvonen, Wang, & Espinoza, 2013), 1,895 students were surveyed and asked to identify both the bully in the school and the "coolest" students in the school. Students identified the same group as bullies and cool kids, which suggest that bullying can raise a student's profile or social status in the school. Students who are bullies are often well liked and receive positive feedback from peers (Salmivalli, 2010). Students who exhibit bullying behaviors are often attempting to dominate the social environment and may even be admired by other students. Bullies may be part of the dominant group such as athletes or other perceived entitled roles within the social hierarchy of the school. The stereotypes of bullies can often mask the behaviors of some students and allows their peer mistreatment to go undetected by school leaders and teachers, as these groups may receive special treatment or allowances. Therefore, it is important that school leaders and teachers avoid a permissive attitude toward certain groups, such as regularly allowing tardiness for the cheerleaders because of a late practice but not for other students who may have legitimate excuses (e.g., they have to ride two city busses to get to school and one is consistently delayed). In addition to breaking the stereotype of bullies as being outcasts or deviants, there is also a lack of research to support that bullying occurs more often with males than females. Bullying occurs at similar rates between both groups, but the types and location of bullying may differ, as boys tend to display more obvious aggressive acts, whereas girls tend to exhibit more verbal threats and relational bullying. According to Tom Snyder, Director of Annual Reports and Information at the U.S. Department of Education, females have higher rates of bullying in the classroom, whereas males reported higher rates of bullying in the locker room and outside on school grounds (Snyder, 2014). Remember, bullies look just like any other student; there is not a set profile.

When I was in elementary school, I had four friends. I accidently hit one in the head. I tried to apologize but she said I was a bully. All my friends turned on me and it lead to me skipping school. I hated life at that point.

Although it is true that students with disabilities can exhibit bullying behaviors, it is more likely that students with disabilities are the victims of bullying and harassment (Swearer, Wang, Magg, Siebecker, & Frerichs, 2012). Students with disabilities who are vulnerable to bullying tend to be socially awkward, be less powerful, have difficulty communicating effectively, and have a low status within the larger peer group. Students may have a visible difference due to traits of their disability: hearing impairment, communication impairment, physical impairment, or other disability-related characteristics that are more noticeable. Victims of bullying may not recognize they are being bullied and may not understand how their behavior affects others within the social group. A student with ASD may repeat the same question every day in class and not adequately read the nonverbal behaviors of their peers who may be annoyed with this behavior. Therefore, bullies and peers may feel the victim is "asking for it" by repeating idiosyncratic behaviors or breaking normal social standards. The research is not entirely clear as to the parameters between the victim and the bully. As such, school professionals should be careful about placing students in a "forever box."

STAFF MISTREATMENT OF STUDENTS WITH DISABILITIES

It is important to acknowledge, although awkward and unpleasant, that adults in a school setting can also exhibit bullying behaviors that create a hostile environment and meet the four-prong threshold set by the U.S. Department of Education, Office of Civil Rights (OCR). Teacher bullying of students in the classroom or on school grounds has received very little critical or peer-reviewed research. There are no national studies on the issue or documented prevalence rates of teacher or adult mistreatment in schools. There is considerable anecdotal evidence that even a small number of adults who exert power, fear, and humiliation over children can do a great amount of harm (McEvoy, 2005). According to Monahan (2013), teachers' actions toward some children can include "persistent criticism, sarcasm, hostility and blaming. It may be that some school personnel use overly harsh disciplinary measures and are unresponsive to the needs of the child" (p. 230). School personnel may lack effective preservice and in-service training for working with students with disabilities, which leads to ineffective and potentially harmful practices in the classroom. As reported by Luke Jackson, a young man with ASD,

> I have to say though that there are some teachers who seem to be bigger bullies than the kids at school . . . Some teachers take great delight in saying things that point out difficulties of kids like me and then bask in the laughter. (p. 142)

Luke makes an important point that educators should recognize: Repeated unwelcome verbal reprimands by a teacher can be bullying or even disability harassment if they create a hostile environment and interfere with the student's ability to benefit from their educational program. For example, consider a classroom teacher who repeatedly reprimands a student with a learning disability by saying the following:

- "Jason, for goodness sake, just once, pay attention."

- "Jason, stop making noises."

- "Jason, what is your problem today? Look at the board."

- "Jason, where is your book again? You would lose your head if it weren't attached."

This constant barrage of unwelcome verbal redirection and unfair treatment from someone with more power directed toward the core characteristics of a disability is not teaching, effectively disciplining, or helping Jason. This type of persistent criticism and sarcasm from the teacher can lead to Jason skipping school and failing grades. For a student with a disability, like Luke Jackson or the fictitious Jason, this continuous and daily treatment can cause serious emotional distress and anxiety and can quickly create a hostile environment.

According to the U.S. Department of Education, Office of Civil Rights, Dear Colleague Letter (DCL; 2013), "It is intolerable for teachers and school staff to be party to school bullying and disability harassment or observers to school bullying." Teachers require training in basic classroom management strategies to positively address student misbehavior and avoid the appearance of harassment or abusive behaviors.

Teacher Remarks About Adult Mistreatment in Schools

I had a colleague who not only bullied students but would often provoke them and get into fist fights with them. I, among many teachers, complained about this man's hateful behavior. Nothing came of it. He had a friend in the superintendent's office who protected him. He was loud, obnoxious, and anti-Semitic. He would often dominate faculty meetings with his jerk behavior. Finally, being no longer willing to tolerate him, I told my principal that I would provoke him and let him see what it's like to take on a fit, 200-pound man instead of a junior high student. The principal told him he no longer had to come to meetings. Being the lazy deadbeat that he was, he happily complied. Many staff thanked me for my action. (Taken from an anonymous online comment at http://www.tolerance.org.)

I have been teased by my fair share of teachers. They shouldn't be teaching. They're supposed to be good role models and protect students. Get your teachers to recognize how unhappy you are; just don't give up.

In addition to the potential negative impact of staff mistreatment for students with disabilities, typically developing students are very sensitive to adult behavior in schools. "Students use information they observe from the teacher to guide social choices. Low preference of a student by a teacher has been found to influence peer rejection" (Monahan, 2013, p. 236). Teacher harassment can have a negative effect on the entire school environment and can create a climate of disrespect and fear. Unfair treatment from an adult in a position of authority, such as belittling a student in the classroom, does not go unrecognized by the other students in the classroom. It supports the belief or culture that students with disabilities are "less worthy" and not valued. As with bullying by classmates, the teacher may not *intend* to harass the student with a disability, but we must recognize that repeated negative verbal reprimands and humiliation that causes harm can be classified as bullying or disability-based harassment. Staff training is a vital component for preventing bullying and harassment in schools. Staff training provides opportunities for school personnel to reflect on their own social and emotional interactions with students and learn effective skills for redirecting mild misbehavior in the classroom. Accountability is crucial to reducing adult mistreatment. Although sometimes difficult, all school personnel must be courageous in the face of student mistreatment by providing constructive feedback to staff who use discriminatory or derogatory language in school. It is up to all parties to not perpetuate the *silence of others.* For more information and resources, consult "Abuse of Power: Most Bullying Prevention Is Aimed at Students; What Happens When Adults Are the Aggressors?" and the free toolkit provided by the Teaching Tolerance web site:

http://www.tolerance.org/abuse-of-power

I used to be bullied in 1st grade because my teacher always yelled at me for being off-task. She even told my parents that I had ADD, but I don't. If they call you retarded, just say "I don't care." I really hope you get help with this problem.

Implementation Checklist

Can you . . . ?	Yes
Review and identify types of bullying	☐
Describe the bully–victim dynamic	☐
Define the differences of male versus female bullying (types and location)	☐
Assess or determine the characteristics of students that are more likely to be victims of bullying	☐
Explain how adults can bully or abuse their power in schools	☐
Summarize the effects of adult mistreatment of students on school climate	☐

The Impact of Bullying
and the School Response

Bullying and harassment cause considerable and lifelong harm to the victim. The peer-reviewed research on bullying and harassment confirms the toll that bullying can take on the roughly 20.4 million students who are affected by or participate in bullying (Srabstein, 2014). Bullying and disability-based harassment has the potential to cause harm, and according to the Centers for Disease Control and Prevention's (CDC's) *Bullying Surveillance Among Youths: Uniform Definitions for Public Health and Recommended Data Elements* (Gladden, Vivolo-Kantor, Hamburger, & Lumpkin, 2014),

> Harm is a range of negative experiences or injuries that can include a) physical cuts, bruises or pain, b) psychological consequences such as feelings of distress, depression or anxiety, c) social damage to reputation or relationship, and/or d) limits educational opportunities through increased absenteeism, dropping out of school, having difficulty concentrating in class, and poor academic performance. (p. 8)

A description of the harm caused by bullying should be highlighted within the school district's definition of bullying and harassment, as the long-term negative impact of bullying on the victim can last into adulthood.

As a student, Luke, very heartbreakingly describes in the example that follows, bullying can leave negative and long-lasting feelings of depression. According to the U.S. Department of Health and Human Services, Substance Abuse and Mental Health Services Administration (SAMHSA, 2014a), bullying is a traumatic event and can leave lasting emotional consequences. Trauma is often associated with family violence, accidents, disasters, or loss, but bullying, like other forms of victimization, can cause trauma. According to Dr. Susan Craig (2008), "Trauma is not an event in

I was bullied since the beginning of school and even after I graduated high school. No one should have to go through the pain and stress that bullying causes. I have a hearing impairment, so I wear hearing aids. When people see hearing aids they know you are different. Now that I have graduated high school I have to live with flashbacks, nightmares, and even a fear of people. I don't have many friends and the friends I have are the only ones I trust. Bullying is a traumatic thing that needs to be stopped before another person dies. I, being a bullying victim, care because no one should have to live through what I had to. (Luke, 18, Georgia; retrieved from the National Bullying Prevention Center, http://www.pacer.org)

and of itself, but a response to an experience so stressful that it overwhelms an individual's capacity to cope" (p. 8). There has been significant study within the fields of mental health and public health on bullying or peer victimization and its impact on children. For school personnel who work in the areas of counseling, psychology, and social work, SAMHSA has a growing body of research and approaches to assist mental health experts and teachers in appropriately responding to trauma (e.g., bullying) with a variety of service delivery options referred to as trauma informed care (TIC). According to SAMHSA's *Treatment Improvement Protocol 57* (2014b), "TIC is a strengths-based service delivery approach that is grounded in an understanding and responsiveness to the impact of trauma that emphasizes physical, psychological, and emotional safety for both providers and survivors" (p. xix). Although the terminology and technical terms utilized in this definition of TIC are slightly different from those typically utilized in the field of education (providers versus teachers), there is much overlap in the mission and goals for both educators and mental health experts. School personnel can draw from the research and findings from the mental health arena in order to formulate trauma-sensitive schools. The Massachusetts Advocates for Children in collaboration with Harvard Law School have written two reports for use by mental health experts as well as school personnel who work directly with students who are victims of trauma:

1. *Helping Traumatized Children Learn: A Report and Policy Agenda* (2005)

2. *Creating and Advocating for Trauma-Sensitive Schools* (2013)

Trauma Sensitive Schools: http://traumasensitiveschools.org/tlpi -publications/

Bullying is a potential traumatic stressor for students with disabilities. The long-term and persistent side effects are associated with substantially worse mental health and leave psychological wounds (Bogart et al., 2014). The effects of bullying can even cause symptoms of posttraumatic stress disorder (PTSD) similar to what was described by Michelle in the preface. A recent research study suggests between 27% and 40% of students who were directly exposed to bullying went on to have potential risk factors for PTSD (Idsoe, Dyregrov, & Cosmovici-Idsoe, 2012). Victims of bullying may display significant levels of anxiety, low self-esteem, and depression and may experience physical ailments (Buhs & de Guzman, 2007; Table 3.1). The American Educational Research Association (AERA, 2013) blue ribbon task force on bullying prevention states that "bullying presents one of the greatest health risks to children, youth, and young adults" (p. 1).

 I have been through the exact thing. What you are feeling is utterly temporary. This will pass, I promise but the self-harm scars on my left wrist for hurting myself are forever. Don't let this make you less of a person. Words will fade, but you will leave a scar in this world if you take your own life. You will regret thinking about death at the age of 30 when you are a mom to a person who loves you. You are somebody.

Each of these consequences of bullying are quite serious, but the senseless acts of children who die by suicide due to a constant barrage of bullying and harassment go beyond the pale of understanding. Bullying and especially chronic bullying has long-term effects on suicide risk and mental health issues (CDC, 2011). Marr and Field (2001) coined the term *bullycide* in their book *Bullycide: Death at Playtime* to highlight the higher rates of suicides among youth as a result of bullying. Since their book was released in 2001, hundreds of cases have been reported from around the world linking teenage suicides to bullying. According to Hertz, Donato,

Table 3.1.   Potential long-term side effects of bullying

- Increased anxiety and panic disorders
- Low self-esteem
- Changes in mood or visible signs of distress
- Depression
- Deterioration of health and overall health problems (e.g., headaches, dizziness)
- Self-harm
- Feelings of alienation and unwillingness to go to school
- Absenteeism
- Substance abuse
- Suicidal ideation

and Wright (2013), bullying behavior and suicide behavior are related, but not all children who are victims of bullying engage in suicidal thoughts or behaviors. There are other risk factors that may contribute to the possibility that a young person will engage in suicide-related behaviors. Other risk factors that may contribute to suicide ideation include mental health factors, environmental influences, and parenting styles. Unfortunately, there are no national data to report the exact number of children or adolescents that turn to suicide to end the nightmare of bullying, but this trend is disturbing and has been a catalyst for many of the latest changes to bullying regulations and policies implemented in schools.

The Study of Epigenetics and Bullying

There are a few preliminary research studies that suggest children who experience long-term and chronic trauma, such as bullying and harassment, may experience long-term genetic implications. The study of epigenetics examines changes in organisms and how environmental triggers can alter gene expression. According to Dr. Sharon Moalem's book *Inheritance: How Our Genes Change Our Lives—and Our Lives Change Our Genes*, "This means, in no uncertain genetic terms, that bullying isn't just risky in terms of self-harming tendencies for youth and adolescents; it actually changes how our genes work and how they shape our lives, and likely what we pass along to future generations" (p. 54). In addition, Vaillancourt, Hymel, and McDougall (2013) go on to suggest "that the experience of being bullied by peers becomes biologically embedded in the physiology of the developing person, which in turn modifies his or her health and, perhaps, learning trajectory" (p. 246). These incredible findings place an additional due diligence on all school personnel to be vigilant when preventing bullying and disability harassment.

 In sixth grade, people started being mean to me. I just ignored it but my grades started dropping. I was failing all of my classes. At the end of sixth grade, I forgot about it over the summer but seventh grade started worse. I was always trying to leave school and one day I was told to die and that I didn't have any friends. I told my mom and the next week I transferred schools. I still get messages from the people that bullied me. I still hear them in my mind and I will never forget the sound of them saying "I hate you." And now I live with the idea that those people still talk about me even though I am not at that school.

IMPACT ON ACADEMIC ACHIEVEMENT

Fortunately most schools and educators are not faced with the tragic loss of a student due to bullying and suicide, but this does not minimize the effect of bullying on the school climate as well as academic achievement. Every school leader and classroom teacher in this country is focused on Common Core standards, high-stakes testing, and student academic achievement. Perform a quick Google search of the keywords "school mission and academic achievement," and it will result in a variety of declarations, such as the following:

- Focus on the core values of high academic achievement.

- Ensure high levels of student performance.

- Create the highest standards of academic excellence.

Unfortunately, with the pervasiveness of bullying in schools, the goal of high academic standards is hindered. Bullying dilutes the quality of education for all students and impairs academic achievement. There have been several studies that suggest a causal relationship between bullying and poor academic achievement (AERA, 2013). The National Education Association (NEA) states that schoolwide bullying has led to poor attendance and decreased academic performance, which also leads to school dropout rates increasing. An estimated 160,000 students miss school every day due to bullying, causing higher rates of absenteeism (Nansel et al., 2001). One study found that victims of bullying had a half letter grade decrease in an academic subject (Juvonen et al., 2011). Victims of bullying are at a higher risk for poor grades and lower school performance (Buhs & de Guzman, 2007; Wang et al., 2014). According to Cohen and Freiberg, bullying in schools undermines student achievement and compromises individual student learning (2013). The impact of bullying causes a loss of concentration and deteriorates educational performance (U.S. Department of Education, 2013). According to the reports from the Massachusetts Advocates for Children's *Helping Traumatized Children Learn* (Cole et al., 2005), childhood trauma, such as bullying, can impede a student's performance in the following areas:

- Language and communication skills

- Problem solving and analysis

- Organization of materials and executive functioning

- Attentiveness to classroom tasks

- Overall engagement in the curriculum

Childhood trauma limits a student's ability to access the curriculum and gain the required competencies for success (Craig, 2008). There is no question that students involved in the bully–victim–bystander dynamic suffer academically and score worse on standardized achievements (Thapa, Cohen, Guffey, & Higgins-D'Alessandro, 2013). For students with disabilities who experience a wide variety of academic challenges, the trauma of bullying is further cause for concern, as it may increase the gap in educational performance. School professionals must recognize that creating and implementing a comprehensive multitiered bullying prevention program not only creates a safe school environment; it also directly affects the overall school mission for high academic achievement.

 I too got picked on for my clothes and music. But it is not a problem for me. Embrace yourself, and everyone else's opinion does not matter. Try to talk to your parents. That has been the most effective solution in my experience. Also, stick up for yourself and laugh with them. I wish the best for you and hope you can settle things.

IMPACT OF PARENTAL INVOLVEMENT

It is important for school personnel to recognize the role of the parent in preventing bullying and harassment in schools. Parents of students with disabilities may experience and exhibit a wide range of emotions, including guilt, powerlessness, and confusion, when collaborating with school personnel. It is important to recognize the additional stress and daily demands placed on parents of children with disabilities. School personnel must work diligently to foster collaborative relationships to meet the needs of the parents and students. According to the Center for Parent Information and Resources (formerly known as NICHCY), "Parents need respect; they need to contribute and feel valued. They need to participate, not merely be involved. It is, after all, the parent who knew the child first and who knows the child best" (2003). Due to the high rates of bullying and harassment for students with disabilities, educators should be proactive and devote greater resources to teaching parents how to recognize, respond to, and report a bullying incident for their child with special needs. Programs that actively engage families within the school community are linked to improved student achievement (Starkey & Klein, 2000). Schools that create a positive school climate and shared partnerships with parents that support cultural diversity experience consistent and positive student academic gains (Dryfoos, 2000).

School personnel must also recognize that parents, regardless of their child's disability, may unwittingly contribute to bullying behaviors due to parenting styles and how conflicts are resolved in the home. There are many environmental and family factors that can increase a student's risk for becoming a bully or the victim of bullying behavior. These variables include domestic violence, drugs and alcohol, and child abuse. Family and parental factors can contribute to bullying behavior (Swearer, Espelage, & Napolitano, 2009). Some parenting styles may also contribute to the bully–victim dynamic, such as exhibiting power and aggression in the home and failing to model appropriate problem-solving skills (Federal Partner in Bullying Prevention Webinar Series, 2013). Some parents may embolden their child to fight back or believe that bullying is a rite of passage. The same is true for those students who are victims of bullying. Some students who have single parents, low socioeconomic status, and families that utilize less authoritative parenting styles have increased odds of being bullied (Swearer, Espelage, & Napolitano, 2009). As previously discussed, there is no stereotype for students who bully, as they may come from different types of families and socioeconomic statuses. It is more important to recognize the overall parenting style and recognize parents who may require additional training and support. School leaders can provide technical assistance and practical strategies that highlight the role of the family and increase resources to build a strong family and community relationships in order to stop bullying in schools.

Parental involvement is an essential feature for creating and implementing a multitiered bullying prevention program (Farrington & Ttofi, 2010). According to the U.S. Department of Education, Office of Civil Rights, Dear Colleague Letter (DCL), parent involvement and training is an effective and evidence-based practice for preventing and addressing bullying in schools (2013). It is important to remember that parental involvement is not a cookie-cutter protocol that is implemented verbatim in each school but a collaborative relationship that is developed through enhanced communication, training, and shared decision making. Parents should be fully involved in the development of an anti-bullying program and empowered to become a full member of the school education team.

 If kids are doing these things, tell your parents. If you don't do anything, they are going to think it is okay. My parents told me, "Don't start it, but finish it."
Y.O.L.O.

IMPACT ON SCHOOL SAFETY

Student safety and school security are a top priority for all school personnel and parents. There is a pressing need for rigid security measures in schools. Many of us remember the "duck and cover" drills of the 1960s, which in present day has warped into lockdown drills. School professionals from the superintendent to office support staff know the importance of putting student safety first and are strictly trained to follow a written protocol for the school's safety plan. Even with these increasing security requirements and the hundreds of millions of dollars spent on school safety and security, the rate of school violence, including guns in schools, has not statistically changed in the last 25 years (Hefling, 2014). According to the executive director of the National School Safety Center, Ronald Stephens, the rate of school associated violence has remained the same, even with the advanced security measures in place. In order to reduce school violence, schools must address the underlying causes and focus on reducing contributing factors such as bullying and fostering student connectedness (Steffgen, Recchia,

& Viechtbauer, 2013). There can be no doubt that bullying is a school safety issue and one of the greatest health risks to children, youth, and young adults (AERA, 2013). Secretary of Education Arne Duncan explains,

> Bullying is ultimately an issue of school safety. Bullying is doubly dangerous because if left unattended it can rapidly escalate to more serious violence and abuse. Just as you have gateway drugs, bullying is a gateway behavior. Too often it is the first step down the road to one of the tragic incidents of school violence we all have watched in horror on the evening news. (2010)

In addition to the U.S. Department of Education's stance on bullying and school safety, multiple national organizations that represent school personnel, from the National Education Association (NEA) and the National Association of School Psychologists (NASP), as well as the Centers for Disease Control and Prevention (CDC, 2014), have written position statements that identify bullying as a threat to school safety and the public health of children. It is time for school leaders and educators to recognize the insidious nature of bullying and its impact on the continuum of school safety. The emerging research in school safety looks to broaden prevention tools and increase a positive school climate (Skiba, 2013). School safety must be redefined to include strategies for preventing and intervening in incidents of bullying and harassment.

 I have experienced a similar situation with bullying. My brother has ADD and used to struggle in school because the teachers wouldn't help him. Don't be afraid to ask questions and find a friend to sit by in school. Try to talk to your principal, that's what I did. Trust me, it was difficult but it stopped the bullying.

IMPACT OF ZERO TOLERANCE POLICIES

Zero tolerance policies and procedures have been widely implemented as a disciplinary response to address student safety since the early 1990s. As tragic school gun violence permeated the media, zero tolerance policies were widely written into state and local school regulations (Skiba, 2013). These school policies focused on severe mandatory punishment for first-time infractions, with quick removal of students through suspension and expulsion. Zero tolerance can, at first glance, appear to be an appropriate reaction for school leaders and the larger school community when faced with school safety and violence. The general policy suggests that for students who possess or use drugs, tobacco, alcohol, and weapons and exhibit other serious behaviors such as vandalism and stealing, the consequences would be harsh disciplinary sanctions including suspensions, expulsions, and referrals to law-enforcement authorities. Zero tolerance policies utilize a tough discipline plan and produce high rates of suspensions and expulsions for first-time offenses. Unfortunately, zero tolerance policies are beginning to spread in schools from their initial use in criminal, gun-related incidents and are now being utilized with increasing attention to bullying and disability harassment. In light of mainstream media coverage of bullying in schools and increased attention on "bullycides," school districts have expanded their zero tolerance policies beyond students who exhibit criminal or violent behaviors to include students who exhibit bullying behaviors. According to the National Parent Teacher Association's (NPTA's) *Resolution Against Bullying* (n.d.),

> National PTA and its constituent organizations endeavor, via educational literature, programs, and projects for parents, students, and school personnel, to bring about an atmosphere of zero tolerance for bullying behavior, and an attitude that bullying behavior is unacceptable and will not be tolerated in homes, schools, playgrounds, buses, school activities, or any place children congregate.

This type of language focuses on a strict punitive policy for bullying and harassment and does not provide evidence-based proactive interventions for the prevention of the underlying causes of bullying in schools. In the case of zero tolerance, the position taken by national organizations such as the NPTA and many school district officials is as follows: If students choose certain behaviors (e.g., bullying), then they must receive adverse and harsh discipline in order to decrease or discourage future incidents of the behavior in order to improve the overall educational environment. However, this strongly worded rhetoric misrepresents the facts and has the opposite effect for student outcomes. According to a DCL sent from the U.S. Department of Education in a joint statement with the U.S. Department of Justice on January 8, 2014, zero tolerance policies have led to decreased academic achievement, increased behavior problems, increased likelihood of dropping out, and increased involvement with the juvenile justice system. According to the NASP (2010), zero tolerance policies are ineffective and in the long run can create unfortunate consequences, such as a racial disproportionality in discipline, elevated dropout rates, and eroded school climate, and negatively affect students with disabilities. The research on the effectiveness of these policies in schools has demonstrated they are ineffective and have failed (Skiba et al., 2006).

In addition to the severe and overly harsh discipline used with such policies, zero tolerance has also resulted in "zero thinking" on the part of school leaders and school personnel (Coloroso, 2008). Cookie-cutter disciplinary policies remove common-sense professional input and limits choices for school leaders addressing the complex social issue of bullying and harassment. These policies provide little room for professional judgment from school leaders when investigating the circumstances around these incidents. Numerous accounts of unwarranted suspensions and expulsions have been reported in the popular media over the last decade:

1. A Hello Kitty bubble gun landed a 5-year-old in school suspension.

2. A 7-year-old boy was suspended for chewing a Pop-Tart into the shape of a gun.

3. A 5-year-old was suspended for making a LEGO gun.

4. A student was suspended for talking about a Nerf play gun.

5. A Nebraska school claimed that a deaf 3-year-old boy's name sign was too similar to "gun."

Although these are extreme cases, they demonstrate what happens when schools are mandated to implement a one-size-fits-all discipline plan with severe punishments. In one instance, a mother anonymously posted the following on a popular social media web site regarding zero tolerance and bullying:

> Zero tolerance is not the way, as life has gray areas. My daughter was defending herself against verbal bullying and pushed a girl's hand out of her face. Because my daughter touched the other student, she was suspended for three days due to zero tolerance policies. She is a straight-A senior with zero prior write-ups, lost her position as a team captain, and has struggled with school ever since.

As this mother clearly explains, zero tolerance policies appear to be spreading from the issues of gun violence to bullying prevention. Schools that falsely rely on zero tolerance policies for stopping bullying in schools have stymied the advancement of research-based interventions for ending bullying and harassment in schools. Instead of expanding these policies, the U.S. Department of Education and U.S. Department of Justice (2014) are suggesting that schools curtail their zero tolerance requirements, as they have not demonstrated significant impact on violence and drug abuse in schools. Therefore, it is not recommended to expand zero tolerance policies for addressing bullying and disability harassment. Although at first glance a strict disciplinary approach to bullying appears to be an appropriate response by school officials and parents outraged due to the harassment toward their children, when you peel back the layers of zero tolerance policies, the reality is that bullying and harassment are complex social issues that require a comprehensive response based on the unique needs of the individual students. Therefore adopting extreme zero tolerance policies for bullying and harassment in schools may have the opposite effect, as increased suspensions and expulsions have no real effect on the rate of bullying in schools. There are alternatives to zero tolerance requirements. State and local policies and programs must include a continuum of predictable graduated consequences for students who exhibit bullying behaviors. As will be discussed in Chapter 9, schools must use their resources to foster student supports, including social-emotional learning, counseling, and addressing the other underlying causes of bullying and harassment.

You have to be strong and speak up for yourself. You got this. You have to remember one thing: You can't make others happy without being happy with yourself. You don't deserve to be called names and it is cruel. You are so much better than them, remember you are strong. P.S. Listen to the song "I Know" by Dude. Hopefully it will help you as much as it has helped me.

Implementation Checklist

Can you . . . ?	Yes
List the four areas that define harm for a student	☐
Define trauma as it relates to bullying	☐
Identify the parameters for trauma informed care	☐
List the long-term effects of bullying and harassment	☐
Explain the role of parental involvement in reducing bullying	☐
Assess your school's zero tolerance policies	☐
Review your school's safety plan. Does it include procedures and protocols for bullying and harassment?	☐

Respond

You are perfect just the way you are. I think you sound like a cool girl who I would love to be friends with. Being different is unique and what makes you the best possible human at your school. Don't change because of the bullies, they are the ones who need to change. You're amazing.

Research-Based Interventions
to Prevent Bullying in Schools

Programs for the prevention of bullying and disability-based harassment vary greatly across different school contexts, demographics, and grade levels, but all programs should include interventions based on scholarly research and evidence based literature. Bullying in schools has been studied both nationally and internationally, beginning in the late 1980s with Dan Olweus. The scholarly research on bullying and harassment has proliferated in the last decade with the onset of numerous state laws and federal guidance letters. There is a growing body of peer-reviewed articles, online resources, and evidence-based interventions that has been published to guide school professionals in developing effective prevention programs (AERA, 2013). For example, a meta-analysis was conducted by Farrington and Ttofi (2010) titled "School-Based Programs to Reduce Bullying and Victimization." The researchers reviewed 44 published anti-bullying programs and identified 20 key elements shared by each of these programs. For a complete list of programs and key features, go to the Campbell Collaboration web site:

---

 http://www.campbellcollaboration.org

In addition to the meta-analysis, the U.S. Department of Education, Office of Special Education and Rehabilitative Services (OSERS), has written a Dear Colleague Letter (DCL; OSERS, 2013) that includes an enclosure titled "Effective Evidence-Based Practices for Preventing and Addressing Bullying." The DCL identifies nine evidence-based practices that are a synthesis of the research and can be applied to all school programs (Table 4.1).

For a copy of the DCL and a complete description of each practice, go to the U.S. Department of Education web site:

https://www2.ed.gov/policy/speced/guid/idea/memosdcltrs/bullyingdcl
-8-20-13.pdf

https://www2.ed.gov/policy/speced/guid/idea/memosdcltrs/bullyingdcl
-enclosure-8-20-13.pdf

NINE CORE COMPONENTS FOR PREVENTING AND RESPONDING TO BULLYING AND DISABILITY-BASED HARASSMENT

Bullying prevention is not an exact science with a standard protocol for every classroom and student, but there are common themes and practices that are applicable across schools. Based on a review of the literature, the Farrington and Ttofi (2010) meta-analysis, and the enclosure from the U.S. Department of Education, I have identified nine common core components for preventing and

Table 4.1. Effective evidence-based practices for preventing and addressing bullying

1. Use a comprehensive multitiered behavioral framework.

2. Teach appropriate behaviors and how to respond.

3. Provide active adult supervision.

4. Train and provide ongoing support for staff and students.

5. Develop and implement clear policies to address bullying.

6. Monitor and track bullying behaviors.

7. Notify parents when bullying occurs.

8. Address ongoing concerns.

9. Sustain bullying prevention efforts over time.

Source: From U.S. Department of Education, Office of Special Education Programs. (2015). *Effective evidence-based practices for preventing and addressing bullying.* Retrieved from https://www2.ed.gov/policy/speced/guid/idea/memosdcltrs/bullyingdcl-enclosure-8-20-13.pdf

responding to bullying and disability-based harassment. Core components refer to "the most essential and indispensable components of an intervention practice or program" (Fixsen, Naoom, Blasé, Friedman, & Wallace, 2005, p. 81).

Many of these core components will be discussed in greater detail in subsequent chapters:

1. *Multitiered interventions:* Bullying and disability-based harassment must be addressed at all levels, from district- and schoolwide policies and initiatives, to classroom-level activities, to individualized targeted interventions. A multitiered flexible framework includes a shared vision for creating a positive school climate, with clearly written policies that include a definition of bullying and identified activities and procedures to prevent bullying and harassment.

2. *Assessment:* Surveys, bullying report forms, and other data collection tools are utilized to monitor and analyze the incidence of bullying and harassment and inform future educational practice. A core component for an effective program includes systematically gathering data to determine the magnitude, scope, and characteristics of bullying and track trends over time with consistent standardized assessment tools.

3. *Positive school climate:* Bullying and harassment interventions are part of the broader goal of establishing a positive school climate where all students, staff, and parents are treated equitably and with respect. A positive school climate supports student connectedness and builds trusting relationships between students and staff.

4. *Social-emotional learning:* Social-emotional learning (SEL) goals and activities are embedded into the curriculum, providing students with daily opportunities to learn social-emotional management, self awareness, problem-solving skills, and interpersonal relationship skills. An SEL curriculum attempts to address the underlying causes of student conflict and teaches a set of skills for social awareness, such as the ability to empathize with others.

5. *Skills-based learning:* Bullying prevention programs teach appropriate skills to students who are vulnerable to bullying, bystanders, as well as students who exhibit bullying behaviors. Individualized interventions include teaching social skills, communication skills, self-advocacy skills, and other skills necessary to reduce the prevalence of bullying.

6. *Staff training:* Professional development defines bullying and harassment and teaches staff to immediately respond to bullying incidents and utilize follow-up procedures such as reporting and investigation. Staff training encompasses disability-based harassment, federal guidance, and the legal ramifications of disability-based harassment.

7. *Parent and community involvement:* An effective program establishes coordinated efforts with parents and community stakeholders. A school safety

team (SST) or anti-bullying task force includes parents, community stakeholders, as well as those individual student groups who are at risk for bullying and harassment. Parental engagement is fostered during each step of a comprehensive program, from communicating the issues of school safety to parent notification of any incidents of bullying or harassment.

8. *Supervise hot spots:* Identifying and improving the supervision of hot spots is an essential component of a bullying prevention program. Bullying can take place anywhere from the bus stop to the classroom, and schools should take precautions when identifying hot spots where bullying is more likely to occur, such as in hallways, on playgrounds, and during extracurricular activities.

9. *Ongoing sustained activities:* The goal of any educational program is implementation, accountability, and sustainability over time. School leaders and classroom teachers must develop and adopt bullying prevention programs and procedures that are sustained to a high degree of fidelity by all staff.

The nine core components for preventing bullying and harassment in schools are not intended to compose an exhaustive list of all research recommendations for what school professionals can implement. The purpose of this list is to provide school personnel easier access to the research, with the hope of greater utilization of evidence-based practices. Local school leaders and classroom-level teachers along with parents and student groups are encouraged to make slight modifications to the core components based on the unique needs of the school environment to ensure long-term positive outcomes. A planning matrix is available in Appendix A to assist school teams in developing an action plan for each of the core components. A rating scale has been developed to allow school personnel to determine the level of implementation of each core component while prioritizing future plans.

In order to implement these nine components consistently across schools, some state educational agencies and school districts have adopted model policies and guidance documents to assist school professionals in bridging the gap between research and everyday practice in schools. These model programs are more than just a brief statement of laws, regulations, or policies but provide school personnel with key outcomes and practical research-based interventions for the classroom. For example, Maine, New Jersey, and Massachusetts have adopted guidance manuals for schools within the state. They include a statewide definition, types of bullying, practices for creating a positive school climate, multitiered interventions, parent information, recommendations for bystander education, and additional resources for effective activities in the classroom (Table 4.2).

These statewide model programs and written guides are available for review by other states or individual school districts as a template for writing a universal framework and procedures to stop bullying in schools. It is not suggested that a written manual prescribe to one program or a cookie-cutter approach for every school to adopt in its entirety. Individual school teams and administrators should be afforded the opportunity to create programs and design curriculum to

Table 4.2. Sample statewide technical assistance guides for preventing bullying and harassment

- Illinois Best Practices in Bullying Prevention and Intervention: http://www.dupage.k12.il.us/main/anti-bullying/pdf/BestPracticesManual.pdf
- Massachusetts Model Bullying Prevention and Intervention Plan: http://www.doe.mass.edu/bullying/#1
- New Jersey Harassment, Intimidation and Bullying: http://www.state.nj.us/education/students/safety/behavior/hib/
- Maine's Best Practices in Bullying and Harassment Prevention: http://maine.gov/doe/bullying/procedures/bestpractices.pdf

meet the unique needs of the student population. A technical assistance guide (TAG) provides teachers and staff with a clear road map for implementing an effective program to reduce bullying. Table 4.3 explains the purpose of a TAG for school personnel.

 High school gets rough, it will get better! My brother was a scrawny little kid and then his junior year he grew and weighs 180 pounds. I am sorry about your clothes, I wish I could give you new clothes. Check out Goodwill, you can find something awesome. I bought a sweater from there and it is cool. Also, when the kids approach you, show no fear. Just don't react. They are insecure and in two years they won't mean a thing.

Table 4.3. What is a technical assistance guide?

A technical assistance guide (TAG) is a generic term used throughout this book to describe a written document developed and disseminated to all school personnel to guide everyday practice in preventing and responding to bullying and harassment. The district or schoolwide team may choose to use a different name for this document. You can call it a manual, a handbook, a framework, or a toolkit. Regardless of the title, the document outlines and provides specific criteria for the core components to effectively and measurably reduce bullying and harassment in schools. A TAG is developed and implemented to ensure strict adherence to federal, state, and local policies and procedures (Swearer, Doces, Jones, & Collier, 2012). Without a TAG or similar document, school leaders and staff are not adequately prepared to stop bullying in schools. Creating a statewide or district-level TAG provides all staff, parents, students, and community stakeholders with the following:

- Clear and compelling rationale for a districtwide bullying prevention program
- Operational definition of bullying and harassment
- Description of core components and evidence-based practices
- Necessary educational resources for implementation
- Socially valid activities and age-appropriate interventions
- Procedural checklists and sustainability measures
- Measurable outcomes for teachers, parents, and students
- Multiple sources of measurement that are objective, transparent, and sustainable

School personnel, pre-K–12, require a universal guide and procedures as a framework for implementing policies with a high degree of accuracy with results-driven accountability.

MULTITIERED FRAMEWORK

State educational agencies, superintendents, district leaders, and teachers take considerable care to secure schools from outside dangerous activities such as drugs, weapons, intruders, weather-related incidents, and even food contamination. Schools commonly implement a multitiered approach to securing schools in order to create a safe and secure learning environment. This multitiered approach begins with a layer of security on school campuses, such as fences surrounding the school property, locked doors, security video surveillance, monitored parking lots, school identification badges, and sometimes metal detectors. All these measures are implemented in order to keep students safe and out of harm's way (Figure 4.1).

No one is arguing the need for multitiered safety measures, but school professionals must also respond to the dangers inside the school that break down safety and security for students. Based on the scholarly research and position statements from influential education associations such as the National Association of School Psychologists (NASP) and the National Education Association (NEA), bullying prevention must be part of the broader multitiered school safety plan. According to the CDC (2014), bullying is one of the most critical issues pertaining to school safety and security. The National Center for Education Statistics' "Indicators of School Crime and Safety: 2012" (NCES, 2013) reports that less than 3% of the public school population is involved with violent crimes, while roughly 20%–28% are involved in the bully–victim dynamic. Although school leaders and teachers must protect students from serious violence and crimes from outside elements, they must also make an investment with a high degree of commitment toward the insidious nature of bullying that breaks down school safety for millions of students every day.

In order for school professionals to ensure student safety, from both outside and within the school walls, addressing and reducing bullying and disability

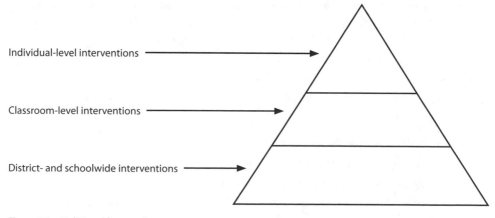

Figure 4.1.   Multitiered framework.

harassment requires a multitiered framework as a core component. As stated by the U.S. Department of Education (2013),

> Evidence-based instructional and intervention strategies for preventing and addressing bullying of students, including students with disabilities, are most effective when used as part of a comprehensive multitiered behavior framework that engages the whole school community. (p. 2)

The multitiered approach suggested by the U.S. Department of Education (2013) was first detailed in a seminal article by Walker et al. in 1996. This initial framework was utilized for preventing and reducing antisocial behavior problems among school-age children and youth with emotional and behavioral disorders. The original model described a three-tiered approach with primary, secondary, and tertiary levels of interventions. This framework has now been expanded and is widely utilized for positive behavioral intervention and supports (PBIS). To read more about the tiered response, review the "Positive Behavioral Interventions and Supports Implementation Blueprint and Self-Assessment":

https://www.pbis.org/blueprint/implementation-blueprint

A multitiered framework provides interventions at various levels of the district and school environment:

1. *District- and schoolwide interventions:* District- and schoolwide practices focus on universal interventions that target the majority of students, including students with disabilities. Focusing strictly on the bully–victim dynamic is not sufficient for addressing the effects of bullying and harassment on the entire school system (Pepler & Craig, 2000). District- and schoolwide approaches for addressing and preventing bullying begin with courageous leaders and district experts who have adopted written universal policies (TAGs), procedures, and protocols for preventing bullying.

2. *Classroom-level interventions:* Responding to bullying in schools requires classroom-level interventions that can be implemented immediately and consistently by highly effective teachers and all school staff. Classroom interventions focus on explicitly teaching anti-bullying skills through inclusive activities within the daily curriculum. Specialized small-group-level or classroom-level strategies involve integrating the curriculum with age-appropriate lessons for SEL skills, bullying awareness, peer mentoring, and bystander education.

3. *Individual-level interventions:* The bystander, bully, and victim require individualized, targeted interventions to meet their unique needs.

Individual-level interventions focus on providing evidence-based supports and services to the bully, victim, and bystander. This level of intervention targets students with disabilities and those students at risk for peer mistreatment.

According to the DCL from the U.S. Department of Education (2013), a multi-tiered framework is aligned and implemented "across each grade level, across special and general education, and in all school settings" (p. 1).

 I am sorry you are going through this. I have not experienced this, but my brother has because he is weak and skinny. Bullying won't stop until college and those dudes will get reality slapped in their face in due time. Take advantage of the fact you are small and make friends with a lot of girls. Girls have this maternal thing, so anyone small is important to them. Your friend.

DISTRICT- AND SCHOOLWIDE INTERVENTIONS

For many teachers and school leaders, it can be tempting to look for a quick-fix program when it comes to preventing bullying and harassment. Compassion and concern for student safety can drive school leaders to start an impromptu anti-bullying campaign by displaying posters around the school, scheduling a one-time assembly, or purchasing a commercial package. Schools are under pressure to quickly create new policies and procedures without careful planning and without the necessary inclusion of all major stakeholders who will ultimately benefit from any adopted program. As these knee-jerk reactions and efforts are understandable when it comes to student safety, these activities may not ultimately achieve the long-term goal of decreasing the incidence of bullying and harassment in schools and creating a positive school climate and safe learning environment for long-term student success. A more cautious and deliberate action plan is formulated when school professionals carefully approach this important issue with strategic planning, assessment, and written measurable outcomes.

The initial steps in developing an effective bullying prevention program begin with a thorough understanding of the research. As discussed earlier, there are thousands of peer-reviewed research articles on the topic of bullying prevention in schools. During the initial stages of implementing the core components of a bullying prevention program, school leaders and others must review the current research with the goal of creating a TAG that describes the activities and essential functions of the program with operationally defined practices and desired outcomes (Fixsen et al., 2005). Without districtwide consistency, schools are left to piece together a fragmented approach with no chance of sustaining positive results.

There are no commercially available bullying prevention programs that will meet the unique needs for every school, every grade level, or every student. "Many programs marketed to schools are not supported by scientific evidence of effectiveness. A program that is compelling may nevertheless have no sustained impact on student behavior" (AERA, p. 57). Therefore, it is important for school leaders to identify staff who are experts on the topics of school safety, creating a positive school climate and developing bullying prevention programs. School personnel in charge of identifying and adopting new educational programs should thoroughly consider all peer-reviewed research and identify programs that are a "good fit" and can be adapted for the unique needs of the student population.

Commercially Available Programs

- *Steps to Respect:* This is a curriculum designed to increase staff awareness and foster social-emotional learning (SEL) and bystander education. This package includes a training manual, DVDs, online support, and student handouts. Available at http://www.cfchildren.org.
- *Olweus Bullying Prevention Program (OBPP):* This program is a multitiered approach that includes school-level, classroom-level, and individual-level interventions. The OBPP program also includes DVDs, school surveys, printable materials, and teacher lessons. Available at www.violencepreventionworks.org.

School personnel responsible for researching and identifying programs can review the Substance Abuse and Mental Health Services Administration's (SAMHSA's) National Registry of Evidence Based Programs and Practices for further commercially available bullying prevention and intervention programs, as it is not the intent of this book to recommend any specific program:

---

  http://www.nrepp.samhsa.gov

Purchasing a prepackaged commercial program does not ensure adequate implementation or measurable sustained outcomes. It is important to remember that preventing bullying and disability-based harassment is not accomplished with a single program and is not a one-size-fits-all model. Schools vary in size, socioeconomic status, diversity, geographical location, and other factors that highlight the importance for a flexible framework and activities that meet the individual needs of the school and students.

I have had a past experience with bullies but I realized that I am not the only one and no one can make me happy. I picked myself up and grew to be a better person than those kids ever were. I wish you well and please remember that things will get better in the future.

Regardless of the adopted program, toolkit, or TAG, it is important that bullying prevention is not seen as another "add-on" policy or an additional requirement for teachers to implement. Core components and coordinated activities are embedded within the overall school improvement plan and ongoing established school safety policies and protocols. It is not uncommon for schools to adopt and implement a variety of new programs within a school year. These programs range from new curriculum programs (e.g., reading curriculum), attendance procedures, counseling or behavioral programs, or computer grading systems. With each additional add-on program, there is a serious risk of a lack of implementation fidelity, adherence to the program, and sustainability over time. As will be discussed in Chapter 9, this is unfortunate because when it comes to bullying and harassment prevention, implementation, fidelity, and sustainability are what matter most when reducing the prevalence of bullying and the harm caused to students. Therefore, when planning and implementing a multitiered prevention program, school leaders should identify current established programs and school procedures in which to embed an anti-bullying agenda. School bullying prevention programs are most effective when they are included as part of the school mission and within the educational environment. For example, most schools have professional school teams that focus on school violence and safety, school improvement plans, academic achievement, and dropout prevention, along with parent-teacher advisory organizations. There is considerable overlap in the missions of these established school groups, through which bullying and harassment prevention can be a thread that weaves them together.

CREATING A POSITIVE SCHOOL CLIMATE

District- and schoolwide interventions that foster a positive school climate create opportunities for strong teacher-student connectedness and respect for all individuals. Creating a positive school climate is a central issue in education today, but unfortunately school climate can be perceived as an add-on or often ambiguous and difficult to objectively define and evaluate. "The vast majority of school leaders do not know, concretely, what school climate reform means," according to Jonathan Cohen, President of the National School Climate Center (2014, p. 1). A positive school climate provides "a blanket of safety, comprehensive enough to cover every space and every person in the school" (Cole, Eisner, Gregory, & Ristuccia, 2013, p. 21). In order for school leaders and teachers to establish a positive school climate, there has to be an accepted common mission and specific action

steps. The U.S. Department of Education (2014) has cited three guiding principles for creating a positive school climate:

1. Create a positive climate and focus on prevention. This principle includes
   developing and implementing a comprehensive multitiered approach
   to creating school safety and security, with written goal statements and
   mission statement to include all stakeholders. Promote social-emotional
   learning with evidence-based teaching practices.

2. Develop clear, appropriate, and consistent expectations and consequences
   to address disruptive student behaviors. Ensure that all staff and students
   are treated with respect, caring, and positive trusting relationships. Support
   the framework of positive behavioral interventions and supports. Involve
   students in all levels of interventions including conflict resolution and social
   problem solving with consistent behavioral expectations. Engage parents in
   school activities and disseminate policies and procedures.

3. Ensure fairness, equity, and continuous improvement. Utilize data-driven
   decision making and continuous improvement plans. Train all staff to
   apply respectful practices and effective classroom management techniques.

Consult the following for more information and to download the U.S. Department of Education's "Guiding Principles: A Resource Guide for Improving School
Climate and Discipline":

http://www.ed.gov/school discipline

Renee Bradley, Project Officer from the Office of Special Education Programs
(OSEP), details explicit features and characteristics that differentiate a positive
school climate from a negative school climate. Table 4.4 is a summary of the
positive and negative characteristics (Bradley, 2014). For a complete review and
to listen to Renee Bradley discuss the differences in school climate, go to the
Federal Bullying Prevention Summit online webcast:

http://edstream.ed.gov/webcast/Play/900a4030cb1249ed99b5f8f693f4e57b1d

A school climate that focuses on creating a feeling of inclusion where
the school is a welcoming environment also benefits students with disabilities

Table 4.4.   Characteristics of a positive school climate versus negative school climate

Positive school climate	Negative school climate
• Predictable, consistent, and equitable treatment • Adults modeling expected behavior • Safe learning environment • Student engagement and participation • Students compliant and cooperative	• Poor leadership • Reactive management • Exclusionary disciplinary practices • Negative adult role models • Students not engaged and disrespectful • Littering, graffiti, vandalism

Source: From Bradley, R. (2014). *How can youth make a difference? Images from youth and young adults that motivated others to make a difference* (PowerPoint presentation). Retrieved from http://edstream.ed.gov/webcast/Play/900a4030cb1249ed9 9b5f8f693f4e57b1d

(Thapa, Cohen, Guffey, & Higgins-D'Alessandro, 2013). Schools that foster a positive school climate begin with goal setting, designing a mission statement, and writing a school improvement plan to meet targeted goals. A mission statement that addresses school climate or a safe learning environment goes beyond a simple motto of "be nice to others" and encourages deeper interpersonal relationships of respect and promotes student learning, school leadership, and connectedness among staff, students, administrators, and parents (Cohen & Freiberg, 2013). A positive mission statement requires input from all stakeholders, including staff, students, parents, and community members. School mission statements describe the essential guiding principles for the school:

1. Schools that foster diversity, respect, and a safe learning environment

2. Educators who are compassionate, dedicated, and treat students with respect

3. Students who possess qualities such as self-confidence and broad-mindedness

The National School Climate Council (2007) has reported that school districts who implement the key principles for a positive school climate have better outcome measures for student achievement and decreased school violence and bullying. Research studies have also revealed that schools that focus on a positive school climate decrease absenteeism, improve student motivation, and have less aggression and bullying incidents (Thapa, Cohen, Guffey, & Higgins-D'Alessandro, 2013). Sadly, schools that do not address bullying within a larger school climate can cause student disengagement and poor academic performance (NASP, 2012).

 This message is for parents and teachers: Students should not feel in danger and alone at school. As the teachers, you should all be "adults" and fix the problem. If bullying is happening, than do something to protect these kids! Sincerely, A concerned friend

Developing and implementing a positive school climate begins with school leaders and classroom teachers who model respectful behavior for all members

of the school community, including students with disabilities. Here are a few practical strategies for school personnel:

1. Get to know every student by name and learn about their families and communities.

2. Spend time in students' homes and attend extracurricular activities and community events.

3. Discuss current events and community issues with students. Share personal experiences with students.

4. Actively listen to student concerns and feedback. Take specific action to let students know their opinions are respected.

A positive school climate is not merely an esoteric, abstract concept that is discussed in scholarly research or written about in the "ivory towers" of a university; it can be measured with a variety of assessment tools such as surveys and student data.

Social-Emotional Learning

Although it is true that developing and implementing a well-articulated and well-planned school mission focused on positive school climate is an important district- and schoolwide intervention for responding to bullying in schools, it may not be enough. Even with a strong ethos of respect and inclusion, students come to school every day with a variety of problems and outside stressors that can limit the success of the school's actions. There are many factors such as poverty, teen pregnancy, food insecurity, community violence, family trauma, and bullying that contribute to feelings of anxiety and interfere with student learning (Cole, Eisner, Gregory, & Ristuccia, 2005). These issues are often barriers to academic success and can minimize a student's ability to effectively access the core curriculum. It is nearly impossible for a teacher to focus on a math or reading lesson if students are not ready to learn and cannot adequately and appropriately manage real-life challenges. Unfortunately, teachers often feel ill-prepared to support the range of problems faced by students and address these social emotional issues while maintaining high academic standards.

In order to assist teachers and students with their concerns over social and emotional issues such as bullying and other school safety issues, statewide educational agencies and school district-level administrators are beginning to incorporate SEL into the classroom curriculum. According to Nel Noddings, a professor at Stanford University and lecturer as part of the Random Acts of Kindness Foundation, SEL

> is not on top of everything else we do in the classroom; it's underneath everything else. The time you spend on caring, kindness, decency, and how we treat one another is so fundamental that everything else goes better as a result. (Noddings, 2014)

A structured SEL curriculum provides every student with the skills for understanding and regulating emotions, developing empathy toward others, cultivating interpersonal relationships, self-management, and managing stress within the structure of the classroom; it allows students a greater opportunity to engage in meaningful learning opportunities. According to the educational agency Collaborative for Academic, Social and Emotional Learning (CASEL), the key elements of an SEL program focus on teaching the life skills that are needed to address student concerns such as bullying or outside stressors. See the CASEL web site for more information, a teacher's guide, and a free webinar for educators:

  http://www.casel.org

According to Nancy Markowitz (2013), an education professor at San Jose State University, "Social emotional learning provides the interpersonal skills students need to perform the academic demands and intellectual tasks of the classroom." An effective SEL program is designed for districtwide interventions from pre-K through 12th grade. Texas, Alaska, Ohio, and California have funded groundbreaking SEL initiatives. In 2004, the Illinois State Board of Education (ISBE) adopted SEL standards for implementation in all grades. The ISBE has written specific educational goals and more than 600 descriptors for student outcomes, beginning with students in early elementary school. The ISBE standards include the following goals for teaching essential skills (Illinois State Board of Education, 2006):

1. *Goal 1—Develop self-awareness and self-management skills to achieve school and life success:* Skills supporting this goal include identifying and managing one's emotions and behavior, recognizing personal qualities and external supports, self-regulation, expressing feelings in a healthy way, and demonstrating skills related to achieving personal and academic goals.

2. *Goal 2—Use social-awareness and interpersonal skills to establish and maintain positive relationships:* Skills supporting this goal include recognizing the feelings and perspectives of others; recognizing individual and group similarities and differences; using communication and social skills to interact effectively with others; and demonstrating an ability to prevent, manage, and resolve interpersonal conflicts in constructive ways.

3. *Goal 3—Demonstrate decision-making skills and responsible behaviors in personal, school, and community contexts:* Skills supporting this goal include considering ethical, safety, and societal factors in making decisions; applying decision-making skills to deal responsibly with daily academic and social situations; and contributing to the well-being of one's school and community.

Evidence from early studies has suggested that schools that have incorporated an SEL program into their curriculum have seen an increase of academic performance, a decrease in the number of problem behavior incidents, and significant improvement in social emotional skills (Durlak, Weissberg, Dymnicki, Taylor, & Schellinger, 2011; Rimm-Kaufman et al., 2014). According to reports from the ISBE (2006),

> SEL programming significantly improves children's academic performance on standardized tests. Moreover, compared to control groups, children who have participated in SEL programs have significantly better school attendance records, less disruptive classroom behavior, like school more, and perform better in school.

For more information, see the ISBE Learning Standards:

http://www.isbe.net/ils/social_emotional/standards.htm

The aim of any adopted school curriculum is to develop positive educational outcomes that teach students to be prepared for the real world and reflect skills needed for post–high school, college, and future employment opportunities. SEL programs not only meet these requirements; they are a district-level intervention that provide universal strategies and learning for all students, including students with disabilities, to effectively respond to bullying and harassment in schools. Practical classroom-level activities for teaching SEL will be discussed in Chapter 5.

School Safety Teams

Decreasing and ending bullying and disability-based harassment requires a high level of commitment from all school staff, students, and parents. School professionals and established education teams should consider assembling a school safety team (SST) to develop grade-level competencies, monitor the implementation of the program, identify necessary supports, and assess outcomes. A SST can assist school district administrators and all staff in writing a comprehensive bullying prevention manual with a variety of coordinated activities, procedures, and standard operating protocols. A SST may be an offshoot of a crisis team, positive school climate team, or school improvement team whose responsibilities include developing anti-bullying initiatives and embedding bullying prevention into the larger mission of the school.

The SST is charged with researching, developing, and implementing the core components for preventing and responding to bullying in schools. For larger school districts, a steering committee or districtwide task force may be involved in defining bullying, identifying a variety of evidence-based prevention practices, writing curriculum, developing surveys, and coordinating professional development. Smaller school districts may decide to create a site-based SST to develop and implement programs and activities. The goal for any team is to incorporate input from all relevant groups and stakeholders within the school community and promote diversity via collaborative partnerships with students, parents, support staff, and community members. It is crucial that students who represent at-risk or vulnerable populations are involved in all levels of a school program and have a voice within the SST. For example, students with disabilities and LGBTQ students should be actively engaged in the SST and have a strong voice in all aspects of developing a bullying and harassment prevention program. It is important for the SST to highlight student-driven activities by eliminating a top-down approach. For example, school leaders should avoid hiring an outside agency to provide a one-time assembly without integral support from a student advisory council or other youth organizations. Students should be involved with making decisions, from the creation of a school motto for a Week of Respect to identifying a school color to represent diversity and kindness.

The SST should do the following:

- Establish and articulate a districtwide definition of bullying that addresses all types of bullying and harassment using current national standards (CDC, 2014). Write and disseminate a TAG with clear policies and protocols that emphasize prevention, positive school climate, and evidence-based interventions embedded at all grade levels.

- Develop a set of coordinated activities that can be implemented throughout the school year. Avoid generic interventions such as "be kind" or "no name calling"; although they might sound positive, they lack an operational definition, are ambiguous, and lead to inconsistent enforcement. Write a list of short-term priorities of student and staff activities while developing long-term initiatives.

- Collaborate with all stakeholders who meet regularly to assess progress and design ongoing anti-bullying initiatives. It is particularly important to invite middle school and high school students to participate in the SST, as they play a vital role in bystander awareness programs. Student involvement as school leaders in an anti-bullying campaign empowers peers and can positively change the social climate of the school (Davis & Nixon, 2014).

- Establish enforcement and high levels of accountability for the adopted written program and develop an evaluation system or implementation checklist for strict adherence by all school personnel.

- Adopt measurable steps for reporting, investigating, and responding to incidents of bullying and provide open, transparent reports to all stakeholders.

- Work collaboratively with other education teams, parent organizations, and community stakeholders when implementing all stages of the bullying prevention program.

- Distribute sample lesson plans for school personnel with a list of goals, activities, and materials necessary to efficiently teach prosocial skills.

- Disseminate high-quality evidence-based resources, web sites, books, flyers, and manuals for staff, students, and parents.

- Collect, analyze, and monitor data that demonstrates bullying policies and programs are implemented effectively. Measurable goals and benchmarks should be reviewed annually as part of the school improvement plan.

- In summary, the SST must enthusiastically champion the sustainability of the adopted policy and program while communicating an inclusive message to all staff and parents.

School shelves are often littered with manuals and school policies. Therefore, it is the task of the SST to ensure that the TAG is not just another manual on the shelf.

 I think you should tell a teacher to do something about the abuse. Maybe sit closer to the front. You are a good person and those kids are mean. Tell a friend to stick up for you and protect you from the bullies. That's what I would do. I hope these ideas help.

PARENTAL INVOLVEMENT

Parental involvement is a core component for a multitiered bullying and harassment prevention program and should be addressed by the SST as part of the TAG. It begins with the inclusion of parent representatives on the SST to ensure collaboration and shared decision making. According to Farrington and Ttofi (2010), parental involvement and parent training are important features in a comprehensive research-based program that can significantly decrease bullying and increase student academic achievement. Assisting parents in becoming effective partners in the fight against bullying and disability harassment requires careful planning and sustained implementation. Planned opportunities are designed by school leaders and teachers to actively engage parents in all areas of bullying awareness, bystander education, and harassment prevention for students with disabilities.

Responding to parents by creating positive parental involvement is not a one-size-fits-all protocol that can be implemented verbatim in every school. Dr. Joyce Epstein, Director of the Center on School, Family, and Community Partnerships at Johns Hopkins University developed a framework to assist school leaders, the SST, and classroom teachers in developing partnerships with parents, families, and community stakeholders. This model is utilized across school districts and at various grade levels to improve and customize parental involvement based on the unique needs of the school and community. For more information, visit the Johns Hopkins University National Center on School, Family, and Community Partnerships web site:

http://www.csos.jhu.edu/p2000/center.htm

Here is Epstein's (2009) framework of the six types of involvement:

1. *Parenting:* Assist families in developing and maintaining a home environment that supports the child and where outside stress is minimized:

   • Provide expert advice on disability awareness and tips about their child's disability.

   • Provide a list of resources and books about disability services in the community and offer materials in other languages (http://www .parentcenterhub.org).

   • Open the school computer lab or school library in the evenings so parents can learn about cyberbullying and programs for Internet protection.

   • Offer parent training and tips on conflict resolution and problem-solving techniques for the home.

   • Provide support and training materials. There are a variety of national and state-level agencies that provide free online training to parents. Parents may be unable to travel to the school site or reluctant to ask for help. Providing easy-to-access online training may be an effective option for parent training and support. For example, the Ohio Center for Autism and Low Incidence offers free online webcasts, resources, and documents for parents to learn about how they can prevent bullying for individuals with special needs:

http://ww.ocali.org

2. *Communicating:* Foster two-way communication using methods that work best for the parent or guardian:

- Survey families to confirm parent contact information and the best methods for communicating effectively (e.g., e-mail, notes home, phone calls, or face-to-face meetings).

- Have teachers make contact with parents at the beginning of the school year to establish communication, share school policies, and answer questions.

- Create and offer less formal events in order for parents to share concerns and receive information and school news (e.g., doughnuts or breakfast with the school counselor or brief open-door office time with the principal or other school leaders).

- Develop flyers, memos, newsletters, and other communications to relay information about bullying and harassment prevention and steps parents can take to intervene.

3. *Volunteering:* Recruit and involve parents and family members to volunteer at school or extracurricular activities and create an atmosphere that welcomes parents and actively seeks parent assistance in schools:

- Invite parents to volunteer to read in the classroom or provide added supervision in hot spots.

- Create and implement a family resource center or academic center that is overseen by volunteers and family members.

- Actively publicize volunteer positions for tutors, boosters, and mentors. Recruit parents for the SST and provide a flexible meeting schedule. Distribute information about volunteering at the school.

- Survey parents for possible needs in the school and identify viable options for parents to contribute through parent organizations such as PTA or to host pizza parties for the student of the month.

- Donate to a library of children's books that focus on diversity and fostering respect.

- Invite parents as guest speakers to discuss a variety of diverse topics and cultural experiences.

4. *Learning at home:* Assist families by providing information about how to effectively help their child at home with homework or other school-related issues such as bullying:

- Create a web site with easy-to-implement bullying prevention and SEL activities.

- Offer after-school tutoring programs on topics geared toward parenting styles.

- Send letters to parents suggesting online resources on how to help their child who may be a victim of bullying.

- Send parents a weekly folder with graded papers so parents can efficiently track their child's progress; include important notices of upcoming events.

5. *Decision making:* Include parents in school decisions, develop parent leaders, and provide opportunities for parents to serve in an advisory capacity:

   - Send letters to parents offering opportunities to serve on the SST or other advisory positions.

   - Conduct surveys to ask parents for specific feedback and guidance on curriculum planning and other school-related issues.

   - Create online networks for parents to express concerns or ideas for those parents who may not be able to attend face-to-face meetings.

   - Seek and identify experts within the parent community who can lobby for school reform and implementation of bullying and harassment prevention programs.

6. *Collaborating with the community:* Coordinate community resources and organizations to strengthen school programs:

   - Publicize on the school's web site and in the local media specific needs of the school and opportunities for professional partnerships.

   - Identify businesses and civic organizations who can contribute to the school's bullying prevention program through donations.

   - Hold a community expo to highlight the resources available in the community for parents and students with disabilities.

   - Solicit pictures, posters, and other appropriate classroom materials that support diversity from parents and community stakeholders.

   - Request printing services of local companies to create posters and stickers.

For a visual representation of parental involvement by researcher Joyce Epstein's work, visit the following site:

 http://www.csos.jhu.edu/p2000/nnps_model/school/sixtypes/6types.htm

Research has demonstrated that parental involvement is an integral part of a bullying prevention program, and the Epstein model provides a framework for engaging parents in meaningful participation in their child's school. Working collaboratively with families and school partners extends connectedness far beyond the classroom walls.

PARENT TRAINING

In order for parents to be fully informed participants and actively engaged, school leaders must guarantee access to high-quality parent training. It involves meaningful active participation in effective practices to assist parents in all areas effecting their child's development (Table 4.5). The goal for parent training is to foster and communicate information with practical tips conveyed in a manner that is compatible with the parent's learning style and preferences.

Parent training is provided at various times that are sensitive to the personal demands of the family, such as travel and work commitments. Online webinars, school brochures, and in-person meetings provide multiple formats for training. In addition to the training format, school leaders should also consider the duration, location, time of day, and topics that are unique to the individualized school community. Surveying parents on preferences for training will assist school staff in creating efficient learning opportunities based on family needs.

In addition to general training on school policies and procedures regarding school bullying, school leaders and teachers should also include specialized training on disability harassment for parents of children with special needs. Typically developing children may have the skills to report bullying (e.g., verbally) to parents or teachers, but some children with disabilities may be unable to report. For students with more severe disabilities and communication delays, it may be impossible to verbally report bullying and harassment to an adult. Therefore, parent training should include information on how to recognize the signs of bullying and how to respond if they suspect their child is a victim of disability harassment. Parent training should focus on identifying signs of victimization and disability harassment (Table 4.6).

Parents know their child best and are keenly aware of unexplained changes. Parents should be trained to be observant of their child's behavior or mood. These signs should never be ignored, and parents should document what they have observed and speak directly with school staff if any concerns arise. Parents play a significant role in working collaboratively with school personnel to decrease bullying in schools and prevent the victimization of students with special needs.

Table 4.5.   Topics for parent training

- Define bullying, harassment, and school policies for prevention.
- Review types of bullying, including cyberbullying.
- Identify effects of bullying and how to recognize the signs at home.
- Teach cultural diversity, tolerance, and acceptable vocabulary.
- Provide tips on how to talk to children about bullying.
- Teach appropriate responses to bullying.
- Provide bystander education.
- Provide reporting procedures for parents and details for follow-up and notification.

Table 4.6. Signs of victimization for students with disabilities

- *Change in sleep or eating patterns:* Is the child eating less, experiencing poor appetite, skipping meals, having nightmares, or not sleeping?

- *Refusing to go to school:* Is the child exhibiting new noncompliant behaviors to avoid school? Does the child tantrum when it is time for school?

- *Unexplained injuries and bruises:* Has the child come home with marks, torn clothes, or cuts that occurred in school?

- *Missing or broken school materials:* Is the child's backpack missing or other school supplies such as books or electronics damaged?

- *Any changes in mood:* Has the child become sullen, adverse to touch, or anxious? Is the child worried, running away, self-destructive, or depressed?

- *Increased aggression at home:* Has the child exhibited increased physical aggression toward siblings or others at home?

School district leaders and the SST should develop and implement systematic and effective opportunities for parents to actively engage in the issues surrounding bullying and harassment prevention and education.

For more information on parent involvement and free training materials, the CDC has developed a guide, fact sheets, and step-by-step activities for promoting parent engagement in schools:

 http://www.cdc.gov/healthyyouth/protective/parent_engagement.htm

STAFF TRAINING

According to research from the NEA, 98% of school staff believe they are responsible for intervening during a bullying incident, but only 46% of those surveyed had received training related to bullying prevention (Bradshaw, Waasdorp, O'Brennan, & Gulemietova, 2013). In addition, only 39% of school professionals were directly involved in developing prevention measures for anti-bullying programs in their schools. Teachers often feel responsible for protecting students in the school but may not even recognize what constitutes bullying behavior. For example, school personnel may have difficulty understanding the various levels of relational bullying, such as 1) damaging someone's reputation, 2) excluding someone, or 3) embarrassing students. Even when teachers believe they are intervening, there can be a discrepancy with student assessment of teacher actions. According to Charach, Pepler, and Ziegler (1995), only 25% of students surveyed indicated that teachers "almost always" intervened to stop bullying. Based on the research, professional development must address the discrepancy between what teachers perceive as intervening and the reality of student observations. In order to increase effective and efficient teacher involvement to prevent and decrease bullying and harassment, school leaders and members of the SST must implement district- and schoolwide professional development and ongoing professional learning communities. All school staff, including administrators, classroom staff, cafeteria and nutrition staff, counselors and therapists, and anyone who interacts with students, require intensive and ongoing professional development to prevent bullying and disability-based harassment.

In addition, school districts are responsible for behaviors or actions by all parties with whom they contract or otherwise delegate responsibility for aspects of the school's program or functions (i.e., coaches or interpreters); training must be developed and implemented for those individuals that may not be directly assigned to the school's campus. According to the DCL (U.S. Department of Education, 2013), all staff should be adequately trained on the legal protections for students with disabilities. In addition, the U.S. Department of Education has stated the following:

> Training is essential in helping school personnel recognize the different forms of bullying that may be directed at students with disabilities and the unique vulnerabilities these students have to social isolation, manipulation, conditional friendships, and exploitive behaviors. (2013, p. 4)

If teachers and staff are explicitly trained in all levels of bullying and harassment and effective interventions, it can greatly reduce the prevalence of bullying and boost academic achievement (AERA, 2014). School leaders and the SST are responsible for providing guidance and training to assist all staff in preventing and responding appropriately to incidents of bullying and harassment. Table 4.7 identifies the overarching goals for staff training.

Table 4.7.   Goals for staff training

- Increase staff awareness and examine their beliefs or stereotypes about bullying and harassment.

- Define bullying and identify potential factors that put students at risk for bullying and victimization.

- Describe the impact of bullying on academic achievement and long-term emotional and mental health effects on the victim. Identify the warning signs of students who experience bullying, especially for students with intellectual disabilities or communication impairment who may be unable to report an incident of bullying.

- Detect the verbal and nonverbal signs of bullying and disability harassment early on, particularly as they relate to relational bullying and other subtle forms of harassment.

- Identify incidents of normal childhood conflict versus bullying and harassment.

- Identify prevention strategies for the classroom and age-appropriate activities to enhance SEL and respect among staff and students.

- Brainstorm curriculum activities and lessons within different curriculum areas; integrate these lessons into other curriculum areas.

- Review and master standard protocols for addressing bullying incidents, including specific reporting measures.

- Coach and model appropriate responses to bullying incidents.

- Review school data and survey assessment tools for shared data-based decision making.

Districtwide training ensures all staff feel secure and confident in their role to prevent and respond to incidents of bullying. Professional development assists staff in identifying examples of bullying and disability harassment, as well as examples of normal childhood conflict and teasing. Again, not all skirmishes are bullying, so it is important to train school personnel to discriminate between lighthearted friendly teasing and bullying:

1. "That shirt is awful," said between two longtime friends.

2. "That shirt makes you look *retarded*," said to a student with a physical disability.

The second statement is clearly bullying and potentially disability-based harassment, and all staff must be trained and committed to intervening immediately. Staff training provides educators with the skills to distinguish between these incidents and be prepared to swiftly respond. A lack of teacher or adult response to mean and harassing statements sends the message that it is okay to name call and gives tacit approval to possible disability harassment and verbal insults. A teacher who does not respond to bullying "colludes with and supports bullying behavior" (Thapa, Cohen, Guffey, & Higgins-D'Alessandro, 2013, p. 6). As reported by the NEA, most school personnel do not receive professional development on how to consistently and effectively respond to an incident of bullying. In a recent survey by Davis and Nixon (2014), one in four students who told adults about a bullying incident were told that if they acted differently, this wouldn't be happening to them. For example, students who received special education services reported that adults were more likely to react negatively in response to bullying such as "ignoring what was going on [or] telling the student[s] to act differently and to solve the problems themselves" (p. 111).

Adequate responses by teachers are considered to be one of the most important components in the district- and schoolwide approach to bullying prevention (Strohmeier & Noam, 2012). Therefore, staff training must include direct instructional practice, coaching, modeling, and feedback of appropriate responses. School leaders and the SST should provide a written standardized protocol as well as follow-up fidelity checklists for all school personnel to follow when observing a bullying incident. For example, the staff protocol can include a simple three-step script for staff to follow at the onset of a bullying incident. For example, consider Stop-Talk-Walk:

1. *Step 1—Stop the incident:*

    •   Stay calm and interrupt the observed student behavior in a firm voice tone. Appear self-assured and stabilize the immediate environment.

    •   Communicate effectively with nonverbal behavior but do not demonstrate overt threatening behaviors such as finger pointing or disrupting personal space.

    •   Make eye contact with the bully and victim.

- Address any immediate safety needs if physical bullying has occurred and remove students who are in danger.

2. *Step 2—Talk to the students:*

- Identify and label the behavior in a direct, neutral voice tone.
- Cite the school rules, code of behavior, and policies violated. Remind students of the written school policies and expectations. For example, "You called her retarded, and that is against the school code of conduct and considered bullying at this school."
- Calmly address the bully but do not criticize or argue the facts. Attempt to deflect any further discussion. Do not drift from the original observed behavior by discussing other incidents. Do not demand an apology, as a student may be agitated and this may escalate the incident.
- Avoid accusations and other statements that can inflame the situation. For example, "What do you think you are doing?"; "Are you causing problems again?"; "Did you call her a whore?"
- Keep the response neutral, on topic, and short. This is not the time to explore the details of what occurred or interview witnesses, as an investigation and follow-up may occur at a future time.
- Teachers are role models for bystanders and the victim on how to respond to a bullying incident with respect; brevity; and neutral, non-threatening body language.

3. *Step 3—Walk away:*

- Direct students to their next destination, which may be the classroom or administrative offices, depending on the severity of the offense.
- Do not touch students when guiding them to exit the scene.
- Ensure the victim is safe and, if necessary, escorted to their destination. Do not completely walk away from the incident or area where the bullying occurred, as continued adult supervision is necessary, but walk away from the one-to-one confrontation with a bully.
- Follow up after the incident and talk to the bully and restate the student code of conduct policies. File a written report if necessary, investigate, determine if disability harassment has occurred, and block any retaliation or further harassment toward the victim (Chapter 8).
- After an incident of suspected bullying, school personnel should reach out to the victim and provide support that includes listening to them and giving advice (Davis & Nixon, 2014). Provide the victim with an opportunity to share their concerns and lend support.

The staff protocol Stop-Talk-Walk is designed to assist adults working in schools a standard response to incidents of bullying. This should not be confused with a program developed by the Office of Special Education Programs (OSEP) in conjunction with Ross, Horner, and Stiller (2008) called the Stop-Walk-Talk program, which is designed for students or bystanders to respond:

 http://www.pbis.org/common/pbisresources/publications/bullyprevention _ES.pdf

An appropriate adult reaction to the bully-victim-bystander incident has a significant impact on decreasing the overall prevalence of bullying and disability harassment in schools (Strohmeier & Noam, 2012). Effective responses to a bullying incident are concise and do not require a long, extended period or discussion; they may only take a few seconds. It may be that a staff member misread a complex social situation or the context of a peer-to-peer interaction. Therefore, a swift, direct, fair, and neutral response may be enough to send a message of respect and remind all those involved that the adults are watching and providing continuous and positive active supervision (Ross, Horner, & Stiller, 2008).

The goal of professional development for bullying prevention is to ensure that all staff are competent in addressing bullying and can intervene quickly and effectively to deter minor rule violations of the school's policy as well as intervene during a bullying incident across all areas of the school grounds. School leaders and the SST must convey to the entire staff the need to be vigilant about student safety. School leaders should identify staff that may be resistant to implementing new strategies based on their prior interactions with students, supporting documents (e.g., numerous office referrals), or stated opinions that "bullying just toughens kids up and is a normal part of childhood." Additional guidance and performance feedback should be provided to staff who have demonstrated limited implementation of the policy and protocol. Teachers should be part of a professional learning community or a mentoring program to staff who may need additional supports such as information from the National Center on Safe Supportive Learning Environments (NCSSLE) and the center's training toolkit for school personnel, "Creating a Safe and Respectful Environment in Our Nation's Classrooms." The training toolkit contains two online modules that address bullying in classrooms with practical strategies for school personnel:

 http://safesupportivelearning.ed.gov/creating-safe-and-respectful -environment-our-nations-classrooms-training-toolkit

Staff Training Methods

High-quality, regularly scheduled professional development and staff training are necessary to reduce the incidence of bullying and harassment. When developing and implementing professional development, the SST and school leaders should carefully consider the type of training and the level of intensity and duration. A one-time, 30-minute after-school lecture to review the school district's anti-bullying policy is not going to provide school personnel with a level of expertise or the mastered skills required to effectively respond to bullying. Staff training is conducted utilizing active participation with multiple sources of information, a written script, and activities such as video examples, lectures, role playing, and direct feedback (Dreiblatt, 2008). As will be addressed in Chapter 9, a lack of adequate and effective training greatly decreases fidelity and ultimately impairs outcomes of potentially effective educational programs (Carroll et al., 2007). If teachers are not highly trained and skilled in addressing and implementing evidence-based interventions to stop bullying in schools and maintaining a positive classroom environment, the program will be deemed substandard and not be sustainable. Without proper supports, school personnel will revert to the adage, "We tried it, and it did not work." According to Bambrick-Santoyo (2010), in order to achieve high standards for program implementation and meaningful professional development, the following steps should be taken:

- Provide lectures that clearly and concretely explain the research, prevalence, and technical language of bullying and disability harassment.

- Enlist content experts in bullying prevention to ensure high quality training. Content experts are familiar with the research on bullying prevention and can translate research into everyday practice for teachers. School district personnel may have difficulty finding a content expert with deep knowledge of bullying and the necessary complex interventions. StopBullying.gov provides guidance for identifying and selecting experts in the field of bullying prevention:

 http://www.stopbullying.gov/news/media/help/index.html

- Provide guided practice with specific examples of evidence-based practices and activities for participation, such as role playing for intervening during an incident of bullying. Provide performance feedback to individual staff who need additional training.

- Reflect on and brainstorm new ideas and opportunities for real-life application to the teacher's classroom with opportunities for feedback.

- Facilitate sharing of personal situations and identify possible roadblocks for implementation, which may include case studies of examples from other school districts with similar student populations. Provide opportunities for creating materials or practicing lessons on bullying prevention.

- Utilize a variety of training formats that include direct educational seminars, mentoring, study groups, professional learning communities, and online webinars. The expansion of educational webinars, podcasts, and other online training events provide an appealing vehicle for school districts to train staff efficiently in bullying and harassment prevention, but a one-time, 60-minute webinar on bullying prevention will not translate into decreased incidence rates of bullying in schools.

Effective bullying prevention programs require high-quality professional development for all staff, conducted regularly.

Girls are bullies. All you need to do is be sarcastic with them and it works! And let me tell you something, you look fine the way you are. Every girl is beautiful inside and out.

ADDITIONAL DISTRICT- AND SCHOOLWIDE INTERVENTIONS

The core components for developing and implementing an effective district- and schoolwide bullying prevention program begin with a written TAG or best practice manual that provides a flexible framework and focuses on procedures for creating positive school climate, implementing SEL activities, the definition and nature of bullying, parental involvement, and staff training. In addition to these key features, the following activities or interventions should also be considered. Most of these practices require little school funding or detract from teacher instructional time:

1. *School web site and technology:* Most schools have a current web site that can be effectively used to publish policies and disseminate procedures for bullying and harassment prevention. The school web site can include specific information for parents and students on the definition of bullying and disability harassment. The school's web site identifies the steps for preventing bullying and harassment in school. According to the U.S. Department of Education (2013), posting the school policy and procedures on the school web site is an effective way to disseminate information on the school's bullying prevention program. The web site has details for reporting a bully as well as appropriate steps for dealing

with bullying in school. Capitalizing on the school's web site to share information does not require any additional funding and allows school leaders to bolster and highlight the importance of creating a safe learning environment. The SST may incorporate other technology-related options for disseminating information across grade levels as appropriate, such as communicating with parents and students via schoolwide text messages to quickly inform parents of upcoming events as well as share important reminders about policies and procedures on bullying and harassment and other school safety issues (e.g., walking safely to school). In addition, the SST can make online short videos or narrated PowerPoint presentations that describe the school's anti-bullying program as well as helpful tips for parents on identifying and responding to signs of bullying.

2. *Schoolwide assembly:* Although a one-time school assembly or a unity day for bullying prevention is not a replacement for a multitiered comprehensive approach, assemblies can bring positive gains for students and staff. Assemblies do not have the far-reaching sustainability needed for bullying prevention, but there are some benefits to a schoolwide assembly. Assemblies are a quick and easy way to infuse enthusiasm into a new initiative. The purpose of the assembly is not to merely review the student code of conduct or create a scare tactic but to send a message of mutual respect and a celebration of diversity. According to Farrington and Ttofi (2010), school assemblies are a core feature for an evidence-based bullying prevention program and can serve to formally announce "the beginning of an intervention program and sensitizing students to new policies" (p. 64). In order to select the most appropriate assembly topic and program, school leaders and the SST, including the students, should 1) preview the performance and check references if paying an outside agency to conduct the assembly, 2) select assemblies with a powerful positive message and engage all stakeholders in participation, and 3) avoid assemblies that send a message that bullying causes suicides or conveys a suicide message, as these discussions are more appropriate in small groups led by highly trained adults who can answer specific and targeted questions (Agatson, 2014). Active student participation is incorporated within all stages of developing a schoolwide assembly. It is important that assemblies are inclusive of students with disabilities, with consideration for accessibility. An anti-bullying assembly may also include a guest speaker who can provide specific details on the effects of bullying and how to stop bullying. Not in Our School, a not-for-profit organization, has created a free online School Assembly Kit for educators. This kit provides a written script for students, PowerPoint presentation slides, videos, and an educator's guide for creating an effective schoolwide assembly that can be adapted for grades K–12:

https://www.niot.org/nios/assemblykit

3. *Pledge drive:* Similar in nature to an assembly, a pledge drive is another schoolwide intervention that does not require any school funds but can create an enormous amount of school spirit and propel students to get involved. For example, Special Olympics has created the "Spread the Word to End the Word" campaign. They have developed an easy-to-implement schoolwide program to get students involved with signing a pledge. Creating an opportunity during lunch or before or after school for every student and teacher to sign a pledge to support the elimination of the word "retarded" is an easy awareness campaign and does not require any instructional time:

http://www.r-word.org

These campaigns are developed as part of student council activities and other community service projects. School leaders should take an active role in pledge drives and take pictures and video of the principal and teachers taking the pledge as documentation of their ongoing commitment.

Talk to your parents and teachers. Tell them you won't accept this behavior from the bullies. Do not accept the label of "retarded." You're more than that. Don't let them define you. Have confidence and also try sitting in the front of the class.

4. *Social media:* In addition to the school web site, many schools have newsletters and other social media sources to share information with students and parents because it is an easy and affordable way to share information with parents (Farrington & Ttofi, 2010). The school newsletter should highlight the school's anti-bullying activities and requests for input, ideas for future events, and words of inspiration from all stakeholders. Ask parents, students, and staff to submit articles or post positive messages to

the school's social media web site. Online social media such as Facebook, Twitter, and other Internet-based resources are an effective and affordable way for the SST and school leaders to increase awareness and share vital information on bullying prevention to parents, students, and staff. The Substance Abuse and Mental Health Services Administration (SAMHSA) created an app called KnowBullying, which provides information to parents on the warning signs of bullying as well as conversation starters for talking to children about bullying:

 http://store.samhsa.gov/apps/bullying

5. *Displays:* Posters of positive messages, banners from the pledge drive, and anti-bullying slogans should visible around the physical environment of the school and created by the students. Commercially bought "Stop Bullying" posters placed in the school hallway are generic and lack student participation. There are plenty of opportunities for students to draw posters, write poetry, create music videos, design a school logo, and other hands-on activities to involve and inspire students in the ongoing mission of creating a safe and respectful school environment. Expressions of respect and anti-bullying campaigns should always reflect the unique traits of the students within the school.

6. *Increased supervision in hot spots:* In addition to these creative and inexpensive activities for students and teachers, school personnel should also establish schoolwide policies for monitoring hot spots as part of an evidence-based anti-bullying program (Farrington & Ttofi, 2010). Hot spots are those physical locations within the school building and outside areas where bullying is most likely to occur. Hot spots include unstructured public areas such as bathrooms, playgrounds, cafeterias, locker rooms, and hallways and extracurricular events where bullying can often go undetected. The cafeteria is often loud, which can mask verbal taunts. The playground is physical by nature, which makes it difficult to spot bullying behavior. According to the 2013 DCL, adult supervision plays an important role in intervening early and modeling expected behaviors. All staff should be vigilant in monitoring hot spots to ensure student safety. The quality of adult supervision can affect students' feelings of anxiety and the overall school climate (Thapa, Cohen, Guffey, & Higgins-D'Alessandro, 2013). According to bullying expert Allan Beane (2009), there are some basic supervision guidelines: Never ignore bullying when supervising public areas, and always scan the public areas; keep a clipboard or other documentation tools to write down any specific incidents;

be focused and pay attention to nonverbal signs of bullying; respectfully remind students of school rules; and do not touch or agitate an angry student. In addition, it may be beneficial to create a copy of the physical layout of the school that identifies these undefined areas and assign specific staff members to supervise and monitor student behavior in these hot spots.

Training staff to take an active role in identifying and supervising hot spots can increase safety and decrease bullying attempts, but the importance of specific training for bus drivers cannot be overstated. Some of the worst behaviors exhibited by students can occur on a school bus. According to the U.S. Department of Education roughly 8 percent of all reported bullying occurs on the school bus (NCES, 2011), and it is the ultimate hot spot. Students take advantage of the lack of supervision, close proximity, and the fact the bus driver is not likely to pull the bus over and take action. School leaders and transportation officials must create and implement effective training for the school bus driver, with guided practice on how to address bullying incidents on the bus as well as procedures to follow up with parents and school leaders. The U.S. Department of Education has developed a bus driver training toolkit called "Creating a Safe and Respectful Environment on Our Nation's School Buses" that is made up of two modules that address bullying on school buses. Specifically, it is designed to assist school bus drivers in cultivating meaningful relationships with students while creating a positive climate on the school bus. For more information and to download a trainer's guide, PowerPoint slides, and handouts, see the following:

 http://safesupportivelearning.ed.gov/creating-safe-and-respectful-environment-our-nations-school-buses-training-toolkit

These practical and effective district- and schoolwide activities are not intended to be an exhaustive list of interventions. School leaders and the SST should actively brainstorm and develop creative student-driven activities that are unique to the needs of the school's student population and community. Involving students and stakeholders in the development of schoolwide interventions will open the door to endless possibilities for effectively responding to bullying and harassment in schools.

Implementation Checklist

Can you . . . ?   Yes

Define multitiered interventions for preventing bullying and harassment   ☐

Foster a positive school climate and list the three guiding principles for
    doing so   ☐

Create a lesson plan for teaching social-emotional learning (SEL)   ☐

List the goals for a school safety team (SST)   ☐

Master the three steps for responding to an incident of bullying
    (Stop-Talk-Walk)   ☐

Plan a school assembly with the student advisory council or youth group   ☐

Increase supervision in hot spots   ☐

Review the six types of parental involvement   ☐

Classroom-Level Interventions

Although it is recommended that district- and schoolwide policies and procedures are thoroughly researched, crafted, and disseminated, this complex level of school improvement planning takes considerable time, with numerous collaborative meetings with staff and stakeholders. Unfortunately, for individual students like Michelle (listed in the preface) and the millions of students bullied in schools, we do not have the time to wait. Classroom teachers must not feel stymied by the slow-moving machine that is educational policy nor continue to perpetuate the *silence of others*. According to Gage, Prykanowski, and Larson (2014), bullying decreased for students who were at high risk when teachers were perceived as trustworthy, caring, and respectful. Teachers must realize the critical role they play in reducing bullying in schools: Individual teachers have the power to help and reduce student trauma and victimization.

The teaching profession is action oriented. Teachers need to be ready to take action and brainstorm concrete practical evidence-based practices for preventing bullying and harassment in schools. According to the National Education Association (NEA, 2010), 98% of teachers surveyed believe it is their job to stop bullying in schools and to be part of the solution for bullying prevention. These teachers and other frontline school personnel such as counselors, related service personnel, and paraprofessionals can make huge gains and positive immediate outcomes when tackling bullying in the classroom level. It has been more than 20 years since Dan Olweus (1993) spoke about the importance of school teachers as the "deciding factors in preventing and controlling bullying activities as well as redirecting such behaviors into more socially acceptable channels" (p. 46). The role and impact of a caring and trusting adult, like a teacher, cannot be underestimated.

Definition of *Teachers*

For the purposes of this text, any reference to "teachers" includes special education teachers and general education teachers as well as other school personnel who provide direct services to students with special needs, such as related service personnel, counselors, and paraprofessionals.

THE ROLE OF THE TEACHER

The success of any classroom-level intervention for bullying and harassment prevention begins with a teacher who is committed to making an investment to stop bullying. One dedicated classroom teacher can enthusiastically lead their class in a positive direction. As with the district- and school-level interventions, classroom-level interventions cost very little in additional school funding but require a high degree of teacher commitment. The first and most important step for teachers is to acknowledge the powerful roles they play in the lives of their students in reducing the incidence of bullying. Successful teachers are role models for teaching tolerance, by demonstrating prosocial skills, and making daily attempts to deepen connections with their students by simply getting to know each student, their interests, and their families.

 I am truly sorry for what you have to go through at school. I understand that school can be a terrible place, especially when you are surrounded by negative people. Talk to your teachers. I have confided in a few teachers and it did help me feel better. Once you start to reach out for help, you will see some amazing changes. Sincerely, Your faraway friend

---

POSITIVE LEARNING ENVIRONMENT

A school assembly, unity day, or the placement of anti-bullying tips on the school's web site are necessary activities for a schoolwide plan for bullying prevention, but the ongoing support of a caring, dedicated teacher helps reinforce a positive learning environment daily. A positive school climate begins with a teacher who practices authentic praise, involves students in classroom decision making, fosters positive relationships, and actively engages students in the learning process. Teachers set the tone of the classroom and determine a safe and civil relationship between all students in the classroom, regardless of ability or special needs. Unfortunately, as previously discussed, teachers and other adults in a position of authority may, even unknowingly, become the bully and harass students with disabilities through repeated unwelcome verbal reprimands and a pattern of conduct that harms the student. There is no question that a small group of students, due to the unique characteristics of their disability, can exhibit challenging behaviors that interfere with the classroom environment and the learning of other students. Mild to moderate behavioral disruptions can include blurting out in class, fidgeting or being out of seat, daydreaming or lack of attention to task, and disorganization with materials. Teachers and paraprofessionals who become frustrated by student misconduct may repeatedly utilize negative verbal reprimands toward students to address minor infractions in the classroom, creating a negative learning environment that leads to the breakdown of the student-teacher relationship. In the Chapter 2 example of Jason, a student with a learning disability, the teacher relied solely on verbal reprimands in front of the entire classroom to redirect Jason's minor behavioral problems. The teacher provided repeated negative and unwanted attention to his disruptions that ultimately only reinforced his behavior through teacher attention and caused other students to have negative perceptions of Jason (e.g., "He is a troublemaker"). Unfortunately, the teacher verbally identified and labeled specific characteristics that were part of his disability: disorganization, inattention, being off task, and impulsivity. "Teachers may justify their behavior as attempts to motivate the student or as appropriate disciplinary actions or just good classroom management" (Sylvester, 2011). Unfortunately, this type of repeated verbal reprimand directed toward a student with a disability is not an effective means of teaching new skills and could lead to feelings of anxiety and teacher avoidance. Therefore, implementing proactive classroom management methods will maintain a positive classroom environment and help the teacher avoid inappropriate reactions to minor classroom infractions.

In order for teachers to nurture student-teacher relationships and maintain a respectful, positive classroom environment, specific classroom management techniques should be reviewed for implementation. Teachers should reflect on the overall classroom environment and ask the following questions:

- Is the climate of the classroom negative, with a high number of verbal reprimands?

- Do students exhibit high rates of off-task behaviors?

- Is the frequency of teacher reinforcement (e.g., social praise) low?

- Do teachers generally feel stressed at the end of the school day? Are they losing patience with specific students?

- Are students with disabilities being pointed out and targeted by teachers for minor infractions?

If the answer to any of these questions is "yes," the following practical strategies for classroom management and establishing a positive classroom environment are recommended for all teachers working in K–12. Implementing these practices with a high degree of fidelity from the start of the school year will ensure a positive learning environment where all students feel safe and ready to learn:

1. Model positive social interactions and respect for all students. Utilize respectful language and voice tone appropriate to the grade level (e.g., high school students do not want to be spoken to as if they were in a Disney movie). Never scream or argue with a student who is exhibiting minor interfering behaviors. Adopting a more positive tone of voice can de-escalate a behavioral situation.

2. Monitor and intervene quickly and efficiently to low-level behaviors (e.g., a student attempting to sleep or text in class). Continuously scan the learning environment and be aware of nonverbal signals and signs of irritation or confusion from students. Determine if any appropriate steps should be taken to intervene (e.g., have the student stand up and participate in handing out class papers, deliver a note to the office, conduct a short lesson on a white board, or take attendance). Keep in mind that some mildly intrusive behaviors should be ignored with planned extinction. Extinction is an evidence-based practice used to discontinue providing reinforcement to a behavior that has been reinforced in the past. For example, a student hums repeatedly during math class, and the teacher verbally redirects the student to "sit quietly" each time. After further assessment and teacher reflection, the teacher determines that his or her verbal redirection has been reinforcing the student by attending to the behavior. The teacher selects to put the behavior on extinction by ignoring the humming in class, as it does not appear to interfere with the learning of other students. Extinction programs are research based when implemented consistently and with treatment fidelity. Inconsistent implementation of extinction programs can cause the behavior to worsen, as students can escalate the minor behavior in order to gain the teacher's attention.

3. Maintain routines and provide productive universal procedures. Standard operating procedures (SOP) are established to teach students how to navigate the classroom structure independently and efficiently. Establish and review procedures that are universal and utilized throughout the school year and applied to both elementary and secondary school classrooms regardless of the nature of the class (e.g., advanced placement calculus versus algebra 1). The class schedule is a critical tool as part of the SOP. The schedule assists students in mastering classroom expectations and allows more efficient and effective transitions. Clearly delineate opening routines; procedures for using the restroom, going to the locker, and turning in homework; and closing activities. In addition, students must be taught how to acquire assistance when needing help or when the teacher is working with

other students. Should they ask a peer, go on to the next task, or sit and wait? SOPs are operationally defined, practiced, and reviewed with all students throughout the school year.

4. Minimize downtime in the schedule. As most teachers learn very quickly, gaps in student engagement and instructional time only further off-task or inappropriate behavior, which may lead to problems in the classroom. Create a schedule with high levels of student engagement and a variety of lessons that maximize time on task. Few students have mastered the skills to sit quietly and wait patiently for the teacher to prepare a lesson or gather materials or for other students to complete a task. Be prepared to have meaningful activities ready for interruptions or for when students finish early. Create three to five interchangeable closing activities that are prepared and distributed if students finish the lesson. A gap in the schedule is a great opportunity to have students work on SEL projects or schoolwide bullying prevention activities.

5. Post rules and expectations. Rules are stated in the positive with examples (e.g., sit quietly during seat work, raise hand to ask questions, remain in seat). Break down each rule into an operational definition and include the appropriate steps. For example, say the rule is to turn in homework. The steps would be as follows: 1) retrieve homework within the first 5 minutes of class, 2) check for completion and name on paper, 3) place homework in the yellow folder on the filing cabinet, and 4) check off name on the homework sheet. Although preparing SOPs requires a time commitment at the beginning of the school year to write down each rule with corresponding steps, it prevents disagreements and confusion throughout the school year when the teacher asks, "Where is your homework?"

6. Create classroom-wide positive reinforcement systems implemented for all students: Focus on teaching prosocial appropriate behaviors and "catch 'em being good." Token economy systems are highly effective and implemented at all grade levels. Elementary school teachers often utilize a sticker when a student provides the correct response to a difficult question and exhibits compliant behaviors, but secondary students are not immune to reinforcement. It is important that teachers working with young adults understand the science of reinforcement and the positive impact on learning. Fake money, poker chips, and colored tickets are an easy way to reinforce students who demonstrate appropriate skills and provide motivation for all students. Tokens are exchanged for simple items or activities such as sitting in the teacher's chair, having extra free time, selecting music for the end of the period, sitting with a friend, being first in line, or receiving special recognition as "student of the week." Provide consistent positive feedback and include written notes home to parents to highlight appropriate student conduct.

7. Develop and post proportional consequences for minor infractions as well as for more serious school offenses. Keep in mind that office referrals result in reduced classroom time and academic instruction and should be used as a last resort (U.S. Department of Education, 2014, p. 6). As will be discussed in more detail in Chapter 6, students who are removed from the classroom for minor infractions are more likely to be suspended or repeat a grade, are less likely to graduate, and may even become involved in the juvenile justice system (U.S. Department of Justice & U.S. Department of Education, 2014). It is imperative to implement comprehensive graduated behavioral interventions to keep students in the classroom via alternatives to office referrals.

8. Provide ongoing feedback with frequent praise. As for the student who is humming in class, the teacher should provide frequent reinforcement for the absence of the humming or for when a student is sitting quietly. Identify students who are following classroom expectations and reinforce this by labeling the intended behavior: "I love the way Jason is looking at me!"; "Excellent work, Sharon, for putting your homework in the yellow folder"; "Way to go, Marshal, for sitting quietly and being patient." Labeling the observable desired behavior while giving positive, genuine praise teaches students appropriate behaviors and classroom expectations. If a teacher limits verbal praise to "good job," the student may be unaware of the targeted acceptable behavior. Teachers should assess the reinforcement system and consistently include all students. Carefully monitor the frequency of social praise: How many times in a class period do you recognize students who are exhibiting appropriate skills? Compare that number (verbal praise) to the number of times you provide instructions and verbally reprimand students. After collecting and analyzing the data, teachers should consider increasing opportunities for students to earn reinforcement as part of the daily routine.

These basic classroom management strategies allow every teacher to maintain a calm, respectful classroom environment where students feel comfortable and ready to learn. There is no question that teachers are faced with a myriad of student behaviors that can interfere with the classroom environment and the learning of other students. Teachers must take great care in addressing the classroom climate and create a safe space where students can learn. Implementing these classroom management techniques with a high rate of fidelity will ensure student success and decrease teacher frustration and create a positive, productive, and efficient classroom where all students are respected and engaged in meaningful learning. Teachers must carefully reflect on their practice and interactions with students to ensure a safe learning environment devoid of any student mistreatment.

It should be noted that students with disabilities who exhibit interfering behaviors that impede learning may require the school multidisciplinary team to conduct a functional behavior assessment (FBA) and write a behavior intervention plan (BIP) as part of the student's individualized education program (IEP) or 504 plan. This type of assessment involves direct data collection, analyzing the function or purpose of the problem behavior, and writing a BIP that teaches alternative or replacement skills. FBAs are effective for determining specific positive behavior supports and accommodations for students who regularly exhibit noncompliance and high rates of misbehavior in the classroom. For additional classroom management interventions, see Appendix B.

 A while ago, maybe when I was in fourth grade, people made fun of me for the clothes I wore. I never had a lot of friends, so no one ever talked to me. I became really sad and depressed. It doesn't help to please others. People will be mean to you and have opinions on the things you do. But now I have an amazing group of friends who helped me get through with my life. When things get bad, I just always remember that things will get better.

SOCIAL-EMOTIONAL LEARNING

As discussed earlier, social-emotional learning (SEL) is a core component for an evidence-based bullying prevention program. A structured SEL program improves school climate and reduces student misbehavior (Durlak, Weissberg, Dymnicki, Taylor, & Schellinger, 2011). SEL programs do not interfere with academic learning but boost academic gains (Rimm Kaufman et al., 2014). An effective SEL program focuses on teaching the essential skills for improving students' self-awareness and the ability to express feelings, interpersonal skills and the importance of diversity, and skills for conflict resolution and decision making. SEL programs can be highly effective in teaching positive behaviors such as respect and social awareness, which then decreases peer conflicts and creates a positive classroom learning environment.

Although some SEL curricula are adopted by the state or local educational agency, classroom teachers can individually incorporate SEL goals into daily lesson plans. At the classroom level, teachers can embed these activities within the standard academic curriculum by focusing on respecting others, teaching tolerance, and student problem solving. Traditional methods for teaching SEL goals in the classroom include lectures, facilitated group discussion, direct instruction, guided practice, role playing, prompting, and modeling. Teachers should structure lessons that provide students with repeated opportunities to practice newly acquired SEL skills with constructive feedback. For example, if students are learning to identify feelings of anxiety or frustration, the teacher can remind students of the steps for reducing stress while making the transition to difficult classes or taking a test.

SEL activities are part of what classroom teachers do every day when guiding discussions on conflict resolution and promoting student self-reliance. According to Dr. Roger Weissberg, President of the Collaborative for Academic, Social and Emotional Learning (CASEL), school personnel can teach SEL skills by following the simple rules of *SAFE* (Weissberg, 2013):

*S*equential activities

*A*ctive learning to practice skills

*F*ocused time on skill development

*E*xplicit targeting of skills

Teachers may choose to write and identify specific times throughout the school calendar to teach SEL skills with planned sequential activities. Initiate educational themes once per month that target emotion regulation, bullying, or interpersonal relationships. Teachers can also create two to three short lessons per month or incorporate guided discussions into language arts and literature, social sciences, and across other curriculum areas.

According to Ruth Cross, Project Director at CASEL (2013), teaching SEL is not always explicit or structured ahead of time. Naturalistic teaching methods expand on real-life situations, providing students with choices, and are often student driven and based on current topics. Naturalistic teaching methods are research based and follow these simple guidelines for implementation (Franzone, 2009):

1. Teachers identify and observe spontaneous discussion or teaching opportunities that occur in a variety of settings. If two students have a verbal conflict in the cafeteria, school staff can take a few minutes to discuss the steps for problem solving and model respectful language.

2. Teachers allow for student-driven topics and the development of ideas. Students identify problems or conflict that occur every day in schools then brainstorm possible solutions. Have students brainstorm problem-solving skills and conflict resolution by sharing ideas and participating in the classroom discussion.

3. Teachers provide guidance and facilitate positive discussions on the various topics that promote the SEL curriculum or similar goals created by the school safety team (SST), such as teaching tolerance and diversity.

4. Teachers may structure discussions around a meaningful quote, ideas from fictional characters, comic strips that exhibit conflict, topical stories from the media, or ideas generated by students.

5. Teachers provide probe questions or forced choices to prompt students who are reluctant to speak up in class discussions: Do you think Lucy should grab the football away from Charlie Brown and watch him fall and then laugh at him? Or do you think Lucy should give Charlie Brown a chance

to kick the ball? What should Linus do when watching Lucy grab the ball? How can Linus stick up for Charlie Brown? Foster students' problem-solving skills and help them with seeking solutions to everyday problems.

6. Spontaneous teaching of SEL goals are utilized by school leaders, counselors, and other support staff throughout the school day when interacting with students in hallways, cafeterias, libraries, and before and after school. Teaching students to take turns, respond positively to others, ask for help, and work as a group should occur many times throughout the school day. School personnel should follow the motto "every space is the right place" for teaching SEL (Weissberg, 2013).

A variety of school personnel can identify teachable moments to discuss topics related to bullying, power imbalance, name calling, and social exclusion to expand the SEL curriculum to all school environments.

Support from the SST is critical for sustainability, with written lesson plans or teacher samples included in the technical assistance guide (TAG) for ease of implementation. The SST should collect, organize, and distribute sample lesson plans created by teachers from within the school or other resources found online, such as on ShareMyLesson.com, which offers lesson plans and resources for K–12 teachers:

 http://www.sharemylesson.com

There are a variety of national organizations that offer free online resources and lesson planning for teachers on SEL activities for the classroom. For example, the Illinois State Board of Education (ISBE) has developed more than 600 specific descriptors to assist teachers in developing lesson plans and teaching SEL for all grade levels. Lesson plans for elementary school should focus on the identification and management of one's emotions and behavior. In a series of lessons, the teacher should address the following:

1. Identify emotions (e.g., happy, surprised, sad, angry, proud, afraid) expressed in "feeling faces" or photographs.

2. Name the emotions felt by characters in stories.

3. Identify ways to calm yourself.

4. Describe a time you felt the same way a story character felt.

5. Discuss classroom and school rules.

6. Share feelings (e.g., through speaking, writing, drawing) in a range of contexts.

These six descriptors can be easily implemented into existing lesson plans and across a wide range of classes such as physical education, art, and music. As part of an art project, students can make a unity chain by cutting strips of paper and having each student write down one word to describe the emotions or feelings that arise when he or she is complimented or praised or when someone supports and helps him or her. Chain the links together and hang the chain around the classroom as a visual reminder of respect and acts of kindness. This project is an easy, efficient, and affordable way to teach about empathy and the importance of interpersonal relationships. For more information on creating a unity chain, visit the National Bullying Prevention Center's web site:

 http://www.pacer.org/bullying/wewillgen/classroom-activities/project -connect.asp

It is important to remember that SEL learning is appropriate and necessary for all grade levels. Middle and high school students require regular teaching and coaching on important social emotional issues as they develop and mature. Adolescents are in need of positive and proactive teaching in order to 1) recognize the feelings and perspectives of others, 2) consider the ethical safety and societal factors in making decisions, and 3) identify and manage emotions and behavior (Illinois State Board of Education, 2004). There are multiple opportunities that arise in a school day that provide opportunities for teaching these important SEL skills to adolescents.

Implementing an SEL curriculum into everyday practice requires additional planning and guidance. The Strong Kids™ program, developed by Dr. Kenneth Merrell from the University of Oregon, is designed for teaching social and emotional skills, promoting resilience, strengthening assets, and increasing the coping skills of children and adolescents. The Strong Kids™ program provides teachers with practical lesson plans, student activities, and handouts for teaching SEL curricula:

 http://strongkids.uoregon.edu/index.html

Not only are SEL lessons important for typically developing students; these practices are particularly important for students with disabilities who may have significant impairments in the social, emotional, and behavioral areas. As will be discussed in Chapter 6, students with disabilities require direct, regular, and concrete teaching of social-emotional goals. By creating everyday opportunities for teaching SEL across settings benefits all students, students with disabilities learn important skills in the general education setting.

 I'm sorry that you have ADD. That must be terrible. People shouldn't bully you for being different, different is better. What if the people bullying you had ADD, the bullies should think about that before they say anything. Sorry you are going threw this. Wish I could help out.

TEACHING BULLYING PREVENTION SKILLS

In addition to incorporating SEL goals and lessons into the daily curriculum, teachers along with support from school leaders, counselors, school psychologists, and social workers should develop and implement structured learning opportunities to teach specific bullying policies and procedures as well as general safety issues for responding to an incident of bullying and harassment. Integrating bullying-prevention lesson plans throughout the curriculum is a core component for an evidence-based prevention program. Interdisciplinary teaching is a way to address social issues, such as relational bullying, with methods that support the generalization of learning discrete skills across other environments. For example, students read about disability awareness in reading class, create a pledge drive as part of a community service project, and speak to younger students on diversity and tolerance. The school's TAG contains the goals for teaching bullying prevention skills to all students. These goals include the following:

- Teach students the definition of bullying and how to recognize signs of bullying behavior. Clearly review the school rules and graduated consequences. Teach common language and vocabulary for the appropriate grade level.

- Provide students with examples to distinguish bullying from normal childhood conflict. Students learn through personal examples. Have students generate different examples of conflict and determine what constitutes bullying.

- Identify types of bullying behavior. Give specific examples of bullying behavior and have students provide concrete scenarios. For example, verbal taunting includes name calling and targeted persistent teasing based on a person's appearance, disability, individuality, race, or ethnicity and other rude verbal comments that can cause harm.

- Teach the steps for recognizing when someone needs help, how to report bullying, and how to support the victim.

- Review school policy and procedures. Have older students train younger students on school policies and procedures through active role playing and scripts. Have older students write a bystander quiz that reviews the school policies, facts, and effective strategies for responding to an incident of bullying. The quiz can be modified for appropriate reading levels and used as a vehicle to discuss possible peer actions. For a sample quiz, review the Eyes on Bullying toolkit:

---

 http://www.eyesonbullying.org

- Teach students the roles and responsibilities of the bystander, including the definition of a bystander and how a bystander can effectively intervene and help victims of bullying and harassment.

- Teach age-appropriate lessons in a variety of formats throughout the school year with regularity. Teachers can develop two or three short activities (15–20 minutes) for implementation on a regular monthly basis. These activities include defining bullying and types of bullying, reviewing school policies, improving bystander awareness, and discussing how to report a bullying incident. As with any new skill, teachers should select multiple methods for teaching each area of the anti-bullying curriculum.

- Sensitize students to the victims in school through cultural diversity activities and by teaching tolerance. Teach empathy and support for other students. Guest speakers or community members from different representative groups should describe personal experiences with bullying and how students can effectively intervene.

- Design instruction in preventing bullying to address different learning styles. Teachers must ensure that students with disabilities are included in the activities.

Introducing anti-bullying education does not take instructional time away from essential academic skills and ultimately decreases minor peer mistreatment and bullying behaviors (Beebe, 2014). Anti-bullying activities can also be integrated across the curriculum via language arts, such as literature, writing projects, and public speaking, as well as social studies, community service projects, art, theater, music, and multimedia projects. For example, community service projects for older students may require students to prepare an anti-bullying flyer and distribute it to elementary schools. Younger students can contribute by developing a school motto or logo for display around the school.

Language arts and literature projects are developed as a vehicle to introduce the concepts and lessons for bullying prevention. According to bullying expert Dan Olweus (1993), "The goal of literature should be to increase the students' empathy with the victims of bullying and to demonstrate some of the mechanisms involved." The use of literature for teaching complex social issues is often referred to as *bibliotherapy,* which is the use of carefully selected books to assist students in problem solving, perspective taking, and appreciating diversity and expand the students' knowledge and attitudes (Gavigan & Kurtts, 2011). Bibliotherapy and the use of age-appropriate literature within the general education classroom for teaching tolerance and anti-bullying procedures is a core component of an evidence-based bullying prevention program (Farrington & Ttofi, 2010). Literature and reading that focus on bullying prevention and tolerance allow students to do the following:

- Build self-awareness of the impact of choices by reading a scenario through the lens of another without criticizing peers or themselves

- Explore multiple perspectives by observing the many sides of the conflict by analyzing literary characters who may suffer adversity and conflict while avoiding quick judgments

- Recognize a world beyond themselves and understand different opinions, alternative choices, and cultural diversity through the characters of a book

There are many language arts resources for school professionals that include specific reading lists and bullying literature for the classroom (Swearer, Espelage, & Napolitano, 2009). Using literature to explore diversity, SEL, and bullying allows the students to feel the characters' emotional states, explore alternatives, and apply the message to their own lives.

Writing activities are another part of the daily curriculum that can be utilized to bolster awareness and teach specific anti-bullying behaviors in the classroom. Lesson plans for writing include poetry, journaling, or writing sample letters to the victims of bullying that include advice. For example, older students can use a "Dear Abby" format to answer questions posed by younger children on how to respond to bullying in the hallways, cafeteria, or on the bus (see examples in Appendix C). This type of structured writing activity uses a format that endorses personal responsibility and creativity, but in a safe medium. Other simple creative writing activities include brainstorming a classroom motto for an anti-bullying campaign. Older students can write and produce a brochure to educate younger students about cyberbullying and online harassment. Writing may also include short stories about past bullying experiences or explanatory text on how to stop bullying in schools. The goal for writing activities is to provide students with a creative outlet for expressing opinions and developing critical thinking skills.

I understand how it may feel like everyone is against you but it's really not. Embrace who you are despite what others are saying. I would recommend to ignore the bullies and to not recognize them in any way. If this does not stop, explain to them that they are hurting you. Hopefully this will help your perspective. Things will get better soon; don't doubt that. Keep your head held high because the future is bright ahead of you.

Multimedia projects allow students to express individualization through technology and the arts. Visual art projects encourage students to explore their feelings about bullying and school safety and increase student engagement and learning by allowing students to choose an appropriate medium. Art and music projects, music videos, and public service announcements through social media may support students' personal reflections on challenges that they may be experiencing in school. Students with disabilities who may experience academic difficulties can focus on art, music, and drawing as an outlet for exploring feelings and experiential learning (Table 5.1). The goals for these classroom-level interventions are to explore the realities of bullying while providing a structured environment to explore the impact of bullying in schools through developmentally appropriate activities.

Mainstream movies, television shows, and documentaries are another powerful medium for supporting teaching efforts in the classrooms. By watching age-appropriate movie clips or current television shows that explore the issues of social exclusion, cyberbullying, and disability harassment, teachers can explore the following questions:

- How are the victims or heroes portrayed?

- Are the characters in the movie realistic? Ask students to think critically about the portrayals.

- What conflicts arise and how are they resolved?

- What choices do the characters make? Evaluate these choices.

Table 5.1.   Projects for exploring bullying prevention in the arts, music, and other forms of media expression

- Music videos on bullying prevention

- Public service announcements for bystander awareness

- Computer-generated images of emotions when victimized

- PowerPoint presentations on conflict resolution

- Posters of the school motto for kindness

- Cartoons to demonstrate kind language

- Poetry that explores diversity

Clips from movies such as *Mean Girls, Harry Potter,* and the classic *Back to the Future* demonstrate a variety of bullying incidents and provide students with an opportunity to reflect and respond to misbehavior in a safe environment through the lens of the character in the movie. Television programs from *Glee* to *The Simpsons* can engage students with powerful images that focus on teaching interpersonal relationships and conflict resolution and help students examine social scenarios from different angles. Using videos that depict bullying scenarios allows students to empathize with the characters while drawing on parallels to their own lives at school. There are numerous movies and television shows that can assist school personnel in showing different perspectives for all grade levels that are age appropriate and safe for school-age students to view. The not-for-profit organization Teaching Tolerance provides educational materials to educators who address diversity in the classroom. Teaching Tolerance offers free downloadable written lesson plans for using movies and television in the classroom and assists school personnel and students in examining stereotypes and differing roles in schools:

 http://www.teachingtolerance.org

In addition to television and movies, a powerful documentary was released in 2011 about bullying in schools. The *Bully* documentary is an examination of the lives of students and parents affected by bullying in schools. The movie provides a raw and emotional account of students who are faced with daily aggression and severe harassment in school. The film is directed by Lee Hirsch, who was a victim of bullying as a child, and empowers communities to engage in the issue of bullying and to positively affect the lives of children in school. The Bully Project offers teachers, parents, and students a variety of materials to support the video as well as practical tools for viewing the movie and multiple activities for students and staff:

 http://www.bullyproject.com

Video or Movies in the Classroom

Teachers should carefully and thoroughly review all videos and movies for appropriate use in the classroom. A list of age-appropriate movies, books, and other video examples surrounding the issue of bullying and harassment should be included in the resources gathered and approved by the school safety team (SST).

Bullying is a terrible thing, but bullies only pick on those they think are weak. So be strong; surround yourself with people who will uplift you, not bring you down. Trust me, there are good people out there. Go kill them with kindness and be confident. Focus on your heart.

CLASS MEETINGS

It is common to find secondary schools providing an advisory period to focus on leadership activities, SEL, goal setting, and other group activities. Elementary schools may refer to these periods as morning meetings or classroom meetings that are regularly scheduled sessions to discuss student concerns, peer mentoring activities, conflict resolution, and communication skills and also highlight prosocial behaviors. Classroom meetings or advisory periods provide an opportunity for the class to share and discuss current issues. Teachers facilitate meetings, but students take a direct leadership role and develop the agenda and topics. Class meetings are an opportunity for teachers to share their own personal stories of childhood conflict and recount times when they felt isolated or victimized by other students. Students enjoy hearing personal stories that allow them to open up about their own experiences. Teachers can follow a few simple rules when implementing class meetings or structured advisory periods:

1. Create a written framework and agenda with time limits that are distributed to students. Create opportunities for students to take on different roles and responsibilities during the meeting (e.g., time keeper, facilitator, secretary).

2. Allow students to research and identify topics for discussion. Teachers can draw from the SEL curriculum or other resources such as those provided by the Teaching Tolerance organization.

3. Facilitate a guided discussion of solutions to current problems, acknowledge different opinions, and attempt to foster consensus within the group.

4. Use positive language and tone and model problem-solving behaviors.

5. Incorporate SEL activities such as stress management techniques.

6. Formulate an appropriate solution and identify evaluation procedures.

A classroom meeting or advisory group is a great way to recognize and reinforce students who have exemplified kindness and respect. Teachers and students identify and share positive experiences or "bucket fillers" (Rath & Clifton, 2004). The "bucket fillers" concept was first described by educational psychologist Dr. Donald Clifton, who created the concept to describe the actions demonstrated by individuals such as kindness, respect for others, patience, and other positive behaviors. The "bucket" represents your mental or emotional self and, when full, it means you are more confident and secure. Classroom activities such as bucket fillers or other classroom-level initiatives that focus on caring and respect provide teachers with an opportunity to identify and teach acts of empathy, caring, and tolerance. Teachers can create a bulletin board or a PowerPoint presentation to show students modeling kindness and acts of caring. Encouraging students to nominate and compliment peers who demonstrate prosocial behaviors is part of the agenda for classroom meetings. According to the Harvard Graduate School of Education's Making Caring Common project, parents and adults who work with children have a key role in developing caring and ethical students. The Making Caring Common project's *The Children We Mean to Raise* recommends focusing on opportunities to practice helpfulness, teaching children multiple perspectives and how to manage feelings (Weissbound, Jones, Ross, Kahn, & Russell, 2014). For more information, visit the Making Caring Common project's web site:

http://sites.gse.harvard.edu/making-caring-common

Another national program designed to promote caring acts of kindness is the Actively Caring for People (AC4P) project. The AC4P is a large-scale movement that aims to establish a more compassionate, interdependent, and empathic culture within schools, businesses, and organizations and throughout entire communities. The positive exchanges between people, resulting from actively caring behaviors and supportive recognition, have a mutually reinforcing effect and lead to an actively caring culture. The AC4P project offers teachers and schools videos and activities to build character strengths and social-emotional competencies in an effort to reduce bullying behaviors in school. These activities and discussions can be included as part of an advisory period or classroom meeting. For more information, visit the AC4P web site:

http://www.ac4p.org

Teachers who promote concepts of caring and empathy through bucket fillers or random acts of kindness reinforce appropriate behaviors and celebrate not only student academic achievement but also the core principles of a positive school climate. Classroom meetings, homeroom, or enrichment or advisory periods are perfect opportunities to address the school's bullying prevention program.

Implementation Checklist

Can you . . . ?   Yes

Identify the principles for a creating a respectful and positive classroom
   environment   ☐

Ensure all students receive positive reinforcement equally throughout the
   school day   ☐

Teach social-emotional learning to students with a focus on emotional
   management   ☐

Promote bibliotherapy for bullying prevention lessons   ☐

Brainstorm acts of kindness for students and staff   ☐

6

Individual-Level Interventions

The top tier of a multitiered framework for preventing bullying and harassment focuses on individualized interventions for targeted groups. These groups require unique interventions that are specially designed and implemented. As discussed previously, the bystander-victim-bully dynamic is fluid and can change throughout the school year or from year to year. For the purposes of this book, we will separate each group and address specific effective interventions, but in reality, these groups overlap considerably. Students who exhibit bullying behaviors may be a bystander to other incidents of bullying. A victim of bullying may turn around and bully other students. School leaders and teachers should understand the various targeted groups and establish interventions for all students. Targeted interventions are not fragmented or separate from the overall school mission of creating a positive school climate and reducing bullying and harassment.

 I know it can be hard watching your friend get bullied at school. But she is your real friend and you need to stand up for her. If she doesn't get invited to parties, then invite her to your own! Don't stand there laughing when she is getting bullied. You must take a stand for her.

THE BYSTANDER

Bullying and disability-based harassment is a school safety issue that not only affects those directly involved in the bullying situation but also negatively affects

the other students in the school. A bystander is someone who witnesses a bullying incident. As mentioned earlier, bullying incidents, which may include physical violence, verbal harassment, and intimidation, frequently occur in front
of peers. Researchers estimate that 85% of bullying occurs with bystanders in
attendance (Pepler & Craig, 2000). In a study by Rivers et al. (2009), 63% of students reported witnessing bullying within the last 9-week period. School leaders, teachers, and parents must recognize the negative impact of bullying and
respond to the large number of students who witness bullying in schools every
day. Just as the victims of bullying can experience negative effects from the direct
impact of bullying, bystanders also experience long-term ill effects. The negative impact for the bystander can range from depression, guilt, anxiety, anger, to
other mental health issues (Rivers, Poteat, Noret, & Ashurst, 2009). Therefore,
it is critical for school personnel to develop and implement an effective bullying and harassment prevention program that includes bystander awareness and
training beginning in the early years of education.

Bystander education is a core component to an evidence-based program,
and with effective training, bystanders can effectively intervene (Polanin, Espelage, & Pigott, 2012; Farrington & Ttofi, 2010). According to Reiney and Harrington
(2012), "When bystanders try to help a bullied child, they are often effective in
stopping it" (p. 39). Whether a school is using a commercial bullying prevention program or has developed its own technical assistance guide (TAG), providing school personnel with the procedures and resources to efficiently teach
bystander awareness is part of the responsibility of the school safety team (SST)
and school leaders.

---

 *If a friend is getting bullied, get up and help them. You should do this the
next time someone says something mean. If they push her down, you go up
to the bully and say, "stop being a jerk what she ever do to you." If you stand
up to them, they will not go after you or your friend ever again. Good Luck.*

When a group of individuals witness a bullying incident and no one inter-
venes, it is referred to by psychologists as the "bystander effect." The bystander
effect is when an individual feels hindered to take action during an emergency.
Responsibility becomes diffused, and the individual is unsure of their role and
responsibility to intervene (Latane & Darley, 1968). The bystander effect occurs in
students who witness bullying in schools. For example, a large group of students
may witness a student with a disability being pushed and called a "retard," but
they fail to stop or intervene during the incident. The bystanders may feel someone else is responsible for intervening or may have feelings of trepidation about
stepping up for the victim. According to a recent study, most students reported
that they would "try to help" during a bullying incident, but only one in four

actually intervened (Syversten, Flanagan, & Stout, 2009). Students in schools are inhibited from taking action when they witness bullying and disability harassment for several reasons, including a lack of awareness and education.

Not all bystanders react in the same manner, and there are a variety of factors that can contribute to the role of the bystander during the bullying incident. Bystanders are sometimes categorized based on different responses to bullying. For example, Olweus (1993) labeled bystanders as *passive, defenders, followers,* or *onlookers.*

- *Passive* bystanders do not take part in the bullying but support the bully by watching and standing around the incident. Passive bystanders do not think that speaking up will help, so they often stand by and watch.

- *Onlookers* shy away from the incident, do not take a position, and attempt to ignore the behavior. As with passive bystanders, *onlookers* may lack the necessary skills to intervene.

- *Followers* will outwardly support the bully and join in with the bully by exhibiting aggressive behaviors, which include name calling or physical aggression. Followers succumb to peer pressure, and they may want to be friends with the bully.

- *Defenders* speak out against a bully and intervene. Some national organizations have labeled the defender role as the *upstander,* as they are standing *up* to the bully.

Whether a bystander is passive or a defender, they may have difficulty understanding their role and level of responsibility to take action. Intervening during an incident of bullying may cause the bystander to be fearful, and they may want to avoid confrontation or retaliation. Bystanders are rightly concerned for their own safety. Alternatively, they may want to improve their own social status within the peer group by joining in as a *follower.* As previously discussed, the bully may be the "cool kid" in school or a popular student. It requires a great deal of skill and confidence to successfully intervene with a student with more power and status. There are valid reasons why a bystander may not intervene, such as fear of retaliation and lack of prosocial skills. Educators must understand the challenging role of the student who witnesses these disrespectful and sometimes aggressive acts.

Bullying is an unwelcome and often repeated behavior that demonstrates an imbalance of power over an individual. However, due to the large number of bystanders viewing the incident, bullying behaviors are often maintained and repeated over time through positive peer influence. Bystanders influence the recurrence of bullying by reacting and reinforcing the bully, even if it is subtle (Salmivalli, 2010). Simply stated, bullies are reinforced by the bystander's attention and reaction to the incident, which gains them even more power (Rose, 2013). O'Connell, Pepler, and Craig (1999) found that 75% of a peer's time is spent providing reinforcement to the bully. Therefore, it is important to empower bystanders and teach them that their individual reaction alone can endorse an act of bullying and even increase further incidents. Laughing at a mean insult or passively watching as a student's backpack is thrown into a school toilet can be interpreted as a way of rewarding the bully. Empower bystanders to be socially responsible and increase their awareness of how their behavior can affect the school's positive school climate and reduce violence against and alienation of other students.

My advice would be to not lose hope. Don't let them get into your head. I am sure there are other students just like you searching for a friend. Also, find a friend who will defend you. Maybe they will punch them for you.

BYSTANDER TRAINING

There are a number of available bystander training programs for students. The Bernese Program Against Victimization in Kindergarten and Elementary Schools (Be-Prox) was designed and implemented in kindergarten programs with highly successful outcomes (Alsaker & Valkanover, 2012). The results of this program have demonstrated significant changes to teachers' attitudes and children's reactions in the presence of bullying. The Committee for Children has developed a research-based program for middle school students, Second Step, which encompasses lessons for bystander training. The program teaches empathy, communication, emotion management, and problem-solving skills in a series of lessons with videos and student practice:

http://www.cfchildren.org/second-step/middle-school.aspx

Another effective bystander training program was developed in Finland and is called the KiVa program. The KiVa program trains students in specific action steps to be implemented when bullying occurs in school by utilizing group discussions and role-playing activities and watching films about how to prevent bullying (Strohmeier & Noam, 2012). The KiVa program is a research-based intervention and can be replicated by other schools with modifications for students with disabilities:

http://www.kivaprogram.net

BYSTANDER PROTOCOL

School leaders along with the SST can purchase a structured prepackaged program or develop a unique bystander protocol as part of their TAG. Similar to a staff protocol, a bystander protocol outlines the possible action steps for the bystander to follow during and after a bullying incident. Without formal training, most students will not speak up or intervene appropriately and safely (Wright, 2003). The most important goal in a bystander protocol is to ensure student safety. There must be a clear understanding in writing that students should not intervene if there is physical violence and/or a possibility for the bystander to get injured. Bystander education programs should deter students from direct aggressive confrontation. It is important that bystanders understand they have options for addressing a bullying incident. Suggesting or requiring students to physically stand up to a bully can cause anxiety in the bystander (Brackett & Rivers, 2014). Developing and implementing a bystander protocol encourages safe student participation and provides simple concrete steps to follow when a student notices a disturbance or a bullying incident. For example, we all remember "stop, drop, and roll" as part of fire safety. The bystander protocol is similarly disseminated and taught to all students with practice sessions throughout the school year.

As mentioned earlier, the Stop-Walk-Talk program developed by Ross, Horner, and Stiller (2008) and the Office of Special Education Programs (OSEP) provides a student or bystander protocol for responding to an incident of bullying. The online toolkit is part of OSEP's Bully Prevention in Positive Behavioral Interventions and Supports (BP-PBS). The program explicitly teaches elementary and middle school students a concrete protocol of what to do if they experience or witness bullying. Stop-Walk-Talk not only is a bystander protocol but also addresses the issue of bullying within the schoolwide positive behavior support model, which includes staff training and ongoing supports. OSEP has also published the Expect Respect program for middle and high school students, with a focus on ensuring that all students and staff are included as part of a schoolwide program of making schools respectful (Stiller, Nese, Tomlanovich, Horner, & Ross, 2013). Both of these online toolkits with staff coaching materials and student lesson plans can be found at the following web site:

 https://www.pbis.org/school/bully-prevention

The most effective bystander education programs explicitly address a range of goals and action steps, such as the following:

- Recognize and detect a disturbance in its early stages. It is important that students understand how bullying starts and what to look for during a bullying incident. What are the verbal and nonverbal signs of aggression or power and domination? Identify phrases that are often used by bullies. Identify hot spots for students where bullying is most likely to occur.

- Intervene and stop the bullying. A bystander education program must teach students to first recognize if they can safely intervene or should instead immediately contact an adult or call the authorities. If a student determines it is safe to intervene, then a set universal protocol is implemented. Discuss intervention strategies such as the hand signal (e.g., hand out in front) used in the Stop-Walk-Talk program. Through guided group discussion, identify age-appropriate skills for intervening. How should a bystander respond? There are a variety of bystander actions that may be appropriate to the given situation. Davis and Nixon (2014) asked students who were victims of bullying to identify the most "helpful peer actions" during an incident of bullying. The majority of students did not want the bystander to directly intervene but instead found the following actions helpful:

  - Spend time with them.

  - Talk to them at school and give them encouragement.

  - Help get them away from the situation.

  - Listen to them.

  - Give them advice.

  - Call them at home.

  - Help them tell an adult.

These results were provided by elementary, middle, and high school students and reveal that victims of bullying seek peer support that includes spending time with peers and helping them get away from the situation. The majority of students responded and identified the need for bystander support as the most helpful action. Therefore, classroom teachers should problem-solve student actions as part of a classroom meeting or advisory period. Teachers are encouraged to brainstorm age-appropriate scenarios and have students role-play a variety of possible responses:

- Foster empathy and provide support for the victim of bullying. Some students with disabilities may exhibit aggressive or interfering behaviors that make it difficult for peers to feel empathy. Students who are victims of bullying have less social status and may not be well liked or popular. Disability awareness programs can teach students about the unique characteristics of individuals with disabilities. Bystander education programs include diversity and tolerance training, which discuss the general characteristics of different disabilities as well as simulation activities to foster a better understanding of the unique differences of others.

- Avoid labeling students as a "bully" during bystander training. Teachers should model caring and respectful language for all students—particularly students who are often rejected by their peers. When teachers demonstrate caring respectful behaviors for all students, there is less rejection of peers who may exhibit aggressive behaviors (Ragozzino & Obrien, 2009; Davis & Nixon, 2014).

- Develop an effective, sustainable bystander education program through annual assessment and student surveys. As will be discussed in Chapter 7, it is important to ask students directly if the program is effective and to identify areas of weakness for continuous improvement and accountability.

Regardless of the bystander response protocol selected by school leaders and the SST, the rules should be short, easy to remember, and applicable to all students. The goal is for all bystanders, including students with disabilities, to understand the steps for responding to a bullying incident and to be able to generalize those skills to the natural environment.

Bystander training will vary greatly based on the age of the students, geographical location of the school, and the unique needs of the student population. School district leaders should develop a bystander education guidance framework and allow the SST and other on-site stakeholders to individualize the program. Schools can select a protocol that is well-matched with a school theme or logo. Bystander education programs for younger students may include a mascot with a puppet show. For example, if the school mascot is a lion, then the steps for a bystander response protocol could be *ROAR*: respond, offer help, use assertive language, and report to an adult. A mascot or catchy theme provides a framework for common language between grade levels and schools. Students in middle and high school are actively involved in the decision-making process for bystander education protocols that are designed with technology or video production. Middle school and high school students can create a motto, such as these frequent slogans found in school hallways: "If you don't report it, you support it," or "Take a stand, lend a hand." These slogans remind students to play a part in talking to an adult about a bullying incident and supporting the victims of bullying and harassment. Embedding the protocol or theme within the daily routine and culture of the school provides for better outcomes and long-term sustainability.

 You should stand up for your friend. Who cares what everybody else says! You should be there for her, even during rough times. I stand up for myself. Even though it is hard because I am tall and have pimples. Right always beats wrong.

Most bystander protocols or lesson plans for bystander training have a component that recommends reporting the incident to an adult. Unfortunately, this runs counter to the long-standing cultural norm of "Do not be a tattletale." Children hear repeatedly from adults during childhood that "no one likes a tattletale." It is up to educators along with parents to redefine what it means to "tattle" versus what it means to be an *upstander*. Part of an ongoing bullying prevention curriculum and bystander training is teaching the difference.

Tattletale versus Upstander

Tattletale—Someone who wants to get someone else in trouble
Upstander—Someone who wants to get a peer out of trouble or be a friend

---

This requires direct instruction with precise examples and nonexamples with guided discussions. Students need to know that it is not okay to go to an adult with the sole purpose of getting someone else in trouble (e.g., "Kathy is chewing gum in class"); they should also know that it is okay to go to an adult if their purpose is to get someone out of trouble (e.g., "Someone threw Jason's backpack in the toilet"). Tattling or telling an adult in order to get someone else in trouble should be discouraged, whereas reporting an incident of bullying should be encouraged. Multiple exemplars are used in teaching to assist and guide students in understanding these concepts or rules that have gray areas. Here are some examples:

- Someone cuts in line in the cafeteria (tattletale).

- Someone has their lunch tray dumped in the trash before they have eaten (upstander).

- Someone has their phone out in class (tattletale).

- Someone has created a fake profile and posted sexual content (upstander).

It is challenging to change a long-held childhood standard about tattling, but educators can begin by teaching common language regarding tattletales versus upstanders as well as by providing specific examples with student-created scenarios. Visual reminders, such as a poster in the classroom, can help to support this message for students.

A variety of instructional methods are utilized for bystander training based on the age and cognitive level of the students. The SST and classroom teacher should individualize all training to ensure the inclusion of students with disabilities. Appropriate accommodations and modifications are made to the adopted protocol and training materials to allow for equal access. As with teaching any new skill to students, regularly scheduled lessons with repetition will increase student outcomes for learning new skills. Literature activities, writing contests, fine art collages, banners, and multimedia projects are an effective, creative way to teach bystanders how to detect bullying behavior and respond to the incident appropriately. Teachers should provide multiple opportunities for students to role-play practice each step of the school-adopted bystander protocol and provide concrete coaching and feedback until students have mastered all necessary steps.

PEER MENTORING

Peer mentoring programs are often created to sustain effective bystander education. The formal engagement of peers is a key element for preventing bullying in schools (Farrington & Ttofi, 2010). Peer mentoring is a structured group to foster diversity and positive peer interactions between students (Janney & Snell, 2006). Peer role models and peer mentoring programs solidify the social norms of the school and have a positive effect on creating a mutually respectful school climate. Research has confirmed that positive peer supports, particularly in secondary schools, significantly reduce bullying victimization (Gage, Prykanowski, & Larson, 2014). It has been demonstrated that peer mentors who are trained to defend the victim reduce the overall impact of victimization and feelings of anxiety, depression, and social isolation (Salmivalli, 2010).

Peer mentoring programs are created utilizing several models. The SST or student advisory council may recruit peers to form partnerships and create a structured group. School leaders and teachers should establish the overall structure of the peer mentoring program and address the following:

- Identify an adult advisor.
- Create selection criteria.
- Recruit students.
- Create an application.
- Conduct interviews.
- Notify parents.
- Provide training and feedback.
- Provide ongoing review of peer mentors.

The Parent Advocacy Coalition for Equal Rights' (PACER's) National Bullying Prevention Center has formed the We Will Generation program, with classroom activities, resources, and suggested videos to educate and inspire students and peer mentors to take positive actions to help their peers. They also have created the "Unite Against Bullying School Event Guide," which provides step-by-step instructions for peer groups and teachers to design and implement a successful bully prevention campaigns. For more information, visit the PACER web site:

 http://www.pacer.org/bullying

Formal peer mentoring programs conduct regularly scheduled meetings and select activities and implement both small and large group events. According to Janney and Snell (2006), the goals for a peer mentoring program are as follows:

- Educate students about diversity.

- Turn student apathy into empathy.

- Focus on proactive team building activities.

- Promote sustainability by passing on the knowledge of older students.

- Understand and communicate the needs of students with disabilities.

- Promote positive attitudes and diversity.

In addition, some peer mentoring programs have been organized specifically for students with disabilities. Students are selected and trained to work with students with disabilities as classroom tutors or social peers during less structured periods of the school day (e.g., lunch, before and after school). For students with disabilities, peer role models and peer mentoring can provide support and assist students when navigating the complex social environment of the school. Some peer mentoring programs recruit older students to take an active role as peer role models for students with disabilities. Best Buddies is a peer mentoring program that focuses on friendships between individuals with disabilities and their peers:

 http://www.bestbuddies.org

These programs offer opportunities for those students who are committed to build positive relationships with their peers by taking social responsibility. Students with disabilities can also mentor younger students who are faced with bullying and harassment. Being a peer mentor can inspire students with disabilities to take an active role in school and boost self-confidence.

Peer mentoring programs strengthen a positive school climate, teaching students diversity and empowering peers to stand together in unity (Carter et al., 2013). There are many resources and organized formal programs for peer mentoring and supports available for school professionals who are actively seeking to create peer mentoring networks. The National School Climate Center has written the "Upstanders in Action" toolkit, which provides lesson plans and training materials to teach diversity and creates opportunities for positive encounters between students with and without disabilities:

 http://www.schoolclimate.org/bullybust/upstander

School leaders can brainstorm with student groups to organize informal peer social groups by utilizing the school name or mascot (e.g., "Langley's Lunch Bunch" or "Robert's Recess Ambassadors") with the goal of *be a buddy, not a bully*. These groups do not follow a set curriculum, hold regularly scheduled meetings, or organize schoolwide events; however, they focus more on fostering friendships in the general learning environment. Some schools have selected tables in the cafeteria, a bench in the courtyard, or designated areas at recess as "friendship zones" where students who may be struggling with the social and communication demands at school can have a safe place to eat and play outside. Regardless of the level of structure of the program, the goal of peer mentoring is to foster caring friendships, support differences, and create opportunities for inclusion and acceptance. These programs are effective and require very little additional funding or instructional time.

You might have to stick up for yourself. Others might not help you because they are afraid of the bullies. Or they could not think of something to say. Teasing is bad but it will get better. Soon you will graduate and get away from it all if you work hard enough. Much love, Your friend

Peer mediation programs are not the same as peer mentoring programs. A peer mediation program trains students in peaceful conflict resolution and offers school personnel an alternative to traditional disciplinary procedures handed down by the teacher or administrator. Some schools have adopted peer mediation programs to address conflicts between students such as bullying. According to the U.S. Department of Education's *Misdirections in Bullying Prevention and Intervention*, bullying is not a conflict but a form of victimization. Mediation may further victimize students who are forced to face the bully. In addition, students with disabilities may not have the necessary communication or adaptive skills to resolve issues face to face and can ultimately be retraumatized by confronting the bully and reviewing the incident(s) that caused the harm. The entire educational brief is available at StopBullying.gov:

http://www.stopbullying.gov/prevention/at-school/educate/misdirections-in-prevention.pdf

STUDENTS WHO EXHIBIT BULLYING BEHAVIORS (THE BULLY)

The labels "bystander," "bully," or "victim," while often used in literature (including this text), can be misleading and should be used with caution. According to

Reiney and Limber (2013), students who exhibit bullying behaviors are not "bad kids"; nor should they be identified with a fixed label. Labeling a student as a "bully" places the onus of the bullying incident on the student without carefully examining larger ecological factors that contribute to bullying and the multiple causes of conflict within the school environment. Because there are many factors that can contribute to a student exhibiting bullying behaviors, school personnel should not apportion blame or find fault with the student but consider other aspects such as school climate, peer influence, and parenting styles.

In addition, some students with disabilities exhibit bullying behaviors. Students may exhibit bullying behaviors due to a lack of understanding of acceptable social behaviors because of an intellectual disability or an impairment of social, emotional, and communication skills. According to Rose, Monda-Amaya, and Espelage (2011), students with disabilities who exhibit bullying behaviors often have impairments in social-communication skills and have learned negative attention-seeking behaviors from their peers. Students with disabilities are at a higher risk to perpetrate bullying behaviors (Maag & Katsiyannis, 2012). According to Rose and Espelage (2012), students with emotional and behavior disorders are at a greater risk for demonstrating bullying behaviors such as aggression, fighting, and other bullying types of behaviors. In another study, 38.1% of students with disabilities said they had bullied other students (Swearer, Wang, Magg, Siebecker, & Frerichs, 2012).

There are several factors that may contribute to a student with a disability exhibiting bullying types of behaviors. Name calling, pushing, and verbal taunting are exhibited by some students with disabilities because these students often have not mastered age-appropriate social skills. According to the Massachusetts Department of Elementary and Secondary Education's "Bullying Prevention and Intervention Resources," students with disabilities are "at risk for being both targets and aggressors. Students may adopt a 'strike first' posture due to having been bullied or excluded in ways that have not been evident to adults" (2011, p. 5). Students with disabilities can also be easily influenced by peer groups and may model the behaviors they observe in the general education environment. According the DCL (2013), if a student who "engages in bullying behaviors is a student with a disability, the IEP team should review the student's IEP to determine if additional supports and services are needed to address the inappropriate behavior" (p. 3). The individualized education program (IEP) team must investigate the reasons or the purpose for the student to exhibit bullying behaviors and may conduct a functional behavioral assessment (FBA), which is a systematic process for determining the functional relationship between a problem behavior and the antecedents or consequences that are maintaining the behavior. The education team then develops a behavior intervention plan (BIP), which is used to provide positive behavior supports and teach alternative and appropriate replacement skills.

If a student does not have an IEP or 504 plan, it may behoove the school team to thoroughly review the student's records and determine if the student may be eligible for special education services and initiate the required actions for Child Find. Child Find is a federal regulation requiring schools to identify and evaluate any student who is suspected of having a disability and in need of special education and related services (IDEA, 2004). If a student is exhibiting high rates of antisocial behaviors, aggression, or other types of bullying behavior, the school multidisciplinary team has an affirmative duty to determine if the child is eligible for special education services and if the behavior is related to a disability. Child Find often targets young children for early intervention services, but the mandate is also applicable to students up to age 21. The impact and symptoms of a disability may change as the student gets older. For example, a young child of 6 years of age receives a medical diagnosis from a neuropsychologist of a mild form of autism spectrum disorder (ASD), but the school multidisciplinary education team, including the parents, determines that the child does not qualify for special education services at that time. Fast forward 5 years and now the child is 11 years of age and demonstrating more severe behaviors, including repeated bullying toward peers. At this point, the IEP team has reasonable knowledge that the student may be eligible for special education services, and through Child Find procedures, the team should reconvene and determine if this student currently qualifies for special education and related services under the Individuals with Disabilities Education Act (IDEA) or section 504.

As previously stated, there are several factors that may contribute to a student exhibiting bullying behaviors in school. School leaders and the SST should broaden the scope of investigating the reasons for high rates of bullying in schools beyond the bully–victim dynamic to include a meaningful examination of other factors that may contribute to the overall bullying rates. Bullying behaviors do not occur in a vacuum, and school personnel must understand that the school environment has a significant role in supporting this behavior. Before the school administration considers punishment for a student who exhibits bullying behaviors, they must first examine and effectively address the school culture and climate as an underlying root cause of the student's behavior. Bullying behaviors are a reflection of the larger social construct of the school, where higher rates of bullying are associated with a negative school environment (Gage, Prykanowski, & Larson, 2014). Has the school developed and implemented specific activities focused on proactive bullying prevention, student-teacher connectedness, and respect for all students and staff? According to the U.S. Department of Education's "Guiding Principles: A Resource for Improving School Climate and Discipline" (2014), school district personnel are advised to engage in "deliberate efforts to create a positive school climate" in order to reduce the need for disciplinary measures when a bullying event occurs. High rates of bullying in a school may be a signal of larger school issues and the need for school improvement planning with implementation of programs and activities with a high degree of commitment and implementation fidelity.

Additional factors contributing to increased bullying behavior can include personal trauma or outside events that negatively affect a student's behavior in the school setting. Violence in the community, a death in the family, or other societal pressures can influence a student's behavior in school. Parental support and awareness are important parts of addressing bullying behaviors in school. Parents need to examine the home environment and talk to their child about bullying. Unfortunately, some students live in violent communities or in homes where parents utilize harsh physical punishment. Parents may be modeling aggressive behaviors, and the student may lack role models for appropriate conflict resolution. Without considering and acknowledging these outside forces, school personnel may not adequately target these larger issues with effective individualized interventions for parents.

I understand your problem. Back in elementary school a kid was my friend and he was bullied too. I did what was right and I stood up to the bully. They didn't bother me after but the bullying of my friend never really stopped. But it wasn't as bad. Pray for the best.

GRADUATED CONSEQUENCES

When examining the disciplinary consequences for students who exhibit bullying behavior, school leaders and the SST should review the policies, procedures, and student code of conduct as it relates to disciplinary actions for bullying. A school policy not only defines bullying but also delineates graduated consequences for students who exhibit bullying behaviors.

Written policies should be carefully reviewed by the SST to ensure they are in compliance with state and federal laws and utilize developmentally appropriate reactive measures. For example, it is not logical to suspend a student for coming to class late; nor is it logical to suspend a student for defending him- or herself against a bully because of a zero tolerance policy. Policies that include disciplinary procedures for students who bully are written in language that is accessible to parents and students. Policies and procedures discussing bullying should be posted in a central location within the school, on the school's web site, and in all materials sent home to parents or guardians. Students and parents may sign a document stating they have read and understand all policies regarding disciplinary actions with regard to bullying and harassment.

School policies and procedures include age-appropriate graduated consequences that support all students and are equally applied. For example, some school procedures for suspension violate federal laws when they unfairly target, even unknowingly, students with disabilities. Students with disabilities are disproportionally suspended at a greater rate than other students. According to a 2014 Dear Colleague Letter (DCL) from U.S. Department of Education and U.S. Department of Justice, students with disabilities "represent 12 percent of the student population, yet make up 19 percent of students who are suspended from school" (p. 1). Strict data collection and record keeping is imperative to ensure that students with disabilities are not targeted for more severe disciplinary measures when exhibiting bullying behaviors in school. School leaders should analyze and monitor monthly and yearly suspensions to ward off any discriminatory practices. For a more information on discipline disparities with practical application to the classroom, read "How Educators Can Eradicate Disparities in School Discipline" (Gregory, Bell, & Pollock, 2014):

---

 *http://www.indiana.edu/~atlantic/wp-content/uploads/2014/03/
Disparity_Interventions_Full_031214.pdf*

Suspension and exclusion from school is a last resort for students who exhibit bullying behaviors. Zero tolerance policies do not make schools safer; they increase school dropout rates, and they dramatically reduce the overall school climate (Skiba, 2013). Punitive discipline measures and zero tolerance policies are counterproductive and are not part of a comprehensive bullying prevention program (Rossen & Cowan, 2012). According to the American Civil Liberties Union (ACLU), "Zero tolerance policies that automatically impose severe punishment regardless of circumstances perpetuate a 'school-to-prison pipeline' which pushes our nation's schoolchildren, especially our most at-risk children, out of classrooms and into the juvenile and criminal justice systems." Traditional school discipline policies are inadequate and are often limited to office referrals, suspension, expulsion, alternative placement, and contact with the juvenile justice system. School leaders and the SST must create alternatives and graduated consequences for students who exhibit bullying behaviors to avoid out-of-school suspensions and a zero tolerance policy.

According to the U.S. Department of Education (2014), "Graduated consequences take into account the developmental differences of students at various stages of childhood and adolescence, as well as the cognitive and emotional maturity of the students served" (p. 14). Graduated consequences begin at the moment a teacher witnesses an incident of name calling, taunting, or bullying type of behavior and sends a clear message that bullying will not be tolerated. The teacher provides immediate verbal feedback to remind students of the code of conduct and school policies. A teacher's consistent, respectful authority can influence future bullying incidents by sending a clear message that bullying or harassing behavior will not be tolerated. A minor offense should be subject to quick and consistent action that is individually tailored to the context of the incident. Inconsistencies with staff responses will create gaps in the overall decline of bullying incidence. For example, if a student yells to another student in the hallway, "You're a fag," then the teacher responsible for supervising the hallway should immediately 1) state the school code, 2) identify the disrespectful language, and 3) intervene using the school's protocol. If later in the school day the same student yells, "You're a fag," in the cafeteria and the two supervising adults 1) roll their eyes, 2) shake their heads in disapproval, and 3) walk away, then these inconsistent responses begin to wear down the fabric of a positive school climate and allow bullying to take hold. It is not recommended for every student who demonstrates rude or disrespectful behavior receive an office referral, but all staff need to be prepared to respond consistently with an adopted protocol at the onset of a bullying incident.

Students who exhibit bullying and harassment behaviors are held accountable for their actions, but harsher punishments are reserved for more violent, repeated, egregious offenses (Table 6.1). There are several variables considered when doling out discipline, and school professionals should investigate all factors before making an appropriate decision. The magnitude, scope, frequency, and nature of the bullying or harassment are carefully reviewed prior to determining disciplinary actions. Strict policies and procedures should not strip administrators and school leaders from making educational decisions that are in the best interest of the individual student while maintaining a safe school environment.

School personnel are required to adhere to federal regulations as they relate to suspension and expulsion of students who exhibit bullying behaviors and are identified as having a disability under IDEA or section 504. Students with disabilities have additional protections, and the school education team may be required to conduct further assessment to determine whether or not the child's behavior that led to the disciplinary infraction is linked to his or her disability. The education team should avoid out-of-school placement options, such as suspension, and review the student's IEP or 504 plan to determine additional supports and services that are needed to address the problem behavior (U.S. Department of Education, 2013). For example, a student with a

Table 6.1. Graduated consequences

- Immediate verbal reprimand or warning
- Contract with the student to "cease and desist" and have no contact with the victim
- Parent phone call to alert them of the incident
- Conference with parent and teacher
- Additional counseling or meetings with the administrator or school counselor
- Alternative lunch detention or in-school lunch suspension
- Student restitution (For example, the student damages school property or another student's belongings such as classroom materials, clothes, or a backpack, so the offending student is responsible for compensating for these items. The form of payment can be individualized.)
- Community service
- Loss of privileges to attend or participate in extracurricular programs
- Before- or after-school detention
- Referral to the school resource officer

disability who has been displaying bullying behavior toward peers at recess may require counseling, social skills training, or modifications to the environment (e.g., increased adult supervision). It is important to remember that students with an IEP or 504 plan have additional civil rights protections and should be afforded due process when faced with any disciplinary measures.

 I know it is tough being bullied; you might think you are alone or can't get through this, but look around at the people who love you and care about you (it helps me sometimes). Also, ask the supervisor on campus to kinda look out for you just in case you can't handle. Hope this advice helps!

Students who repeatedly exhibit bullying behaviors and do not respond to traditional measures, such as conferencing with a trusted adult, may require additional supports or a referral for specialized services. Students identified as chronic bullies may exhibit more severe psychological problems and require additional supports from mental health experts. School psychologists or counselors can provide cognitive behavior therapy to help students examine their own thoughts and emotions, recognize negative thoughts, and use strategies to change their thinking and behavior. Individualized interventions include counseling to manage aggression, teaching coping skills, teaching empathy, stress management, and family training. Anger management skills focus on emotion regulation, perspective taking, and direct discussion with students on how to manage normal childhood anger (Swearer, Espelage, & Napolitano, 2009). Parental involvement is incorporated within the graduated consequences to the greatest extent possible. Successfully dealing with serious and chronic acts of bullying is not a short-term process but part of the long-term "educational goal for helping students become lifelong learners, productive workers, and contributing citizens" (Fink, 2014, p. 5).

THE VICTIM

Despite the growing national attention toward preventing bullying and harassment in schools and the strongly worded guidance and technical assistance of the U.S. Department of Education (2000, 2010, 2013, & 2014), school districts are still lagging with implementing a multitiered comprehensive prevention program and interventions specifically designed for students with disabilities. Students receiving special education services were at a high risk for bullying and reported increased rates of bullying (Rose, Swearer, & Espelage, 2012). Students may exhibit behaviors that tend to trigger peer mistreatment, like repeating questions, breaking social rules, displaying irritating habits, or dressing differently. This is not to say that bullying is excused, but it is important to thoroughly investigate factors of bullying in order to create comprehensive prevention programs for students with disabilities. Several national studies have confirmed that students with physical disabilities who receive special education services are more likely to be bullied (Davis & Nixon, 2014). Yet a paucity of research on evidence-based methods specific for addressing students with special needs exists within the bullying literature (Young, Ne'eman, & Gelser, 2011). "Unfortunately, there needs to be much more investment in research that examines the unique bullying dynamics surrounding vulnerable populations" (AERA, 2013). The majority of school-based bullying prevention programs are written and developed for students in the general education setting. School district personnel can modify and adapt the core components for an evidence-based program with additional interventions for students with disabilities.

All school personnel who work with students with disabilities should be highly trained in understanding the federal protections provided by law for students with disabilities and closely follow the laws and guidance letters (OCR, 2000, 2010, 2014; OSERS, 2013). School district personnel are responsible for protecting students from physical or emotional harm and for eliminating a hostile environment (OCR, 2010). When responding to the victims of bullying and harassment, school district personnel must first ensure that students with disabilities are protected from a hostile educational environment and have an effective IEP that provides a free appropriate public education (FAPE).

Ability Path is an online hub of resources for parents and professionals who support individuals with disabilities. They have developed and made available "Walk a Mile in Their Shoes," a toolkit that provides specific research and recommendations to prevent disability-based harassment. This toolkit is an excellent resource for training school professionals about federal regulations related to disability-based harassment:

http://www.abilitypath.org/areas-of-development/learning--schools/ bullying/articles/walk-a-mile-in-their-shoes.pdf

If you think you are weird, embrace it. We are all weird. Friends can make it better. Don't be ashamed to tell your parents or find another adult. I promise someone will listen and care, just like me. I truly believe you can overcome this hardship and shine through the clouds.

INDIVIDUALIZED EDUCATION PROGRAMS OR 504 PLANS

The school district, in conjunction with the parents, must take steps to address the issues of victimization by convening the education team and reviewing the student's IEP or 504 plan. According the U.S. Department of Education, Office of Special Education and Rehabilitative Services (OSERS; 2013), and the Office of Civil Rights (OCR; 2014), the school should convene the IEP team or 504 team to determine the necessary aids and services for a student who has been a victim of bullying on any basis. The education team, which may include the general education teacher, special education teacher, speech and language therapist, occupational therapist, school administrator, parents, and the school counselor, must conduct formal and informal testing to determine the current baseline for a student's Present Level of Academic Achievement and *Functional Performance* (PLAAFP) as it relates to a student receiving FAPE (IDEA, 2004). The U.S. Department of Education defines *functional performance* as "skills or activities that are not considered academic or related to a child's academic achievement." This term is used in the context of routine activities of everyday living, such as social and communication skills, problem-solving skills, critical thinking skills, and skills for developing interpersonal relationships. The education team should examine not only the academic needs within the general education environment but also the social-communication and behavioral needs for the student to access the general education environment. When discussing a student who has been a victim of bullying or disability-based harassment, the education team should include a statement of strengths and weakness in the area of functional performance. Present levels reflect the necessary supports and services to prevent harassment and ensure FAPE not only in the classroom but also in the student's interactions with peers in the cafeteria, hallway, extracurricular activities, and school bus. For example, a student with an intellectual disability may have difficulty making transitions with large groups in the hallway, may be isolated from peers during physical education, and may be secluded at lunch. The education team should objectively assess the impact of this type of social exclusion and determine if the student is obtaining meaningful educational benefit based on the current baseline data (U.S. Department of Education, 2013). For example, a student may be repeatedly taunted and harassed on the bus in the morning on the way to school, which causes increased outbursts and high levels of anxiety and interferes with the student's ability to learn and benefit from their educational program throughout the school day. All information written into the IEP or 504 plan should be current; data driven; and based on formal testing, evaluation data, and direct observations. The objective information written in the PLAAFP provides the foundation for writing goals, selecting services, and ultimately determining placement for the student.

Although an IEP and 504 plan are written based on the individual needs of the student, it should be noted that with the high rates of bullying and victimization for students with disabilities, the education team can reasonably assume that a student with a disability may, in all likelihood, be confronted with verbal or physical taunting and possible disability-based harassment. Therefore, the education team should consider if the student has been a victim of bullying and address concerns within the IEP or 504 plan. In 2010, Massachusetts passed legislation that addresses bullying, harassment, and teasing in public schools. According to the Massachusetts Bullying Prevention and Interventions Resources web site, "If a student is vulnerable to bullying the IEP team will determine accommodations, services, and interventions needed to help the student develop skills to prevent and stop bullying."

http://www.doe.mass.edu/bullying/considerations-bully.html

It would behoove all states and school education teams to follow Massachusetts's lead in adding an additional special factor for all students with disabilities. Special factors are included as part of IDEA (2004; PL 108-446), which requires the IEP team to consider certain additional supports or factors for students with disabilities (Table 6.2).

Although the federal government does not currently require special considerations for bullying or harassment as part of its regulations, state and local educational agencies are allowed to add statements or requirements to an IEP or 504 plan. Given the high rates of bullying for students with disabilities and the severe long-term consequences, all education teams for students with disabilities should add the following special factor: "If a student is vulnerable to bullying, the team will determine accommodations, services, and interventions that are needed to prevent bullying and obtain a FAPE." The education team should then write measurable goals for teaching:

Table 6.2.   Individuals with Disabilities Education Improvement Act (IDEA) special factors (section 300.324[a][2][i]–[v])

Consideration of special factors. The IEP Team must—

(i) In the case of a child whose *behavior* impedes the child's learning or that of others, consider the use of positive behavioral interventions and supports, and other strategies, to address that behavior;

(ii) In the case of a child with *limited English proficiency,* consider the language needs of the child as those needs relate to the child's IEP;

(iii) In the case of a child who is *blind or visually impaired,* provide for instruction in Braille and the use of Braille unless the IEP Team determines, after an evaluation of the child's reading and writing skills, needs, and appropriate reading and writing media (including an evaluation of the child's future needs for instruction in Braille or the use of Braille), that instruction in Braille or the use of Braille is not appropriate for the child;

(iv) Consider the *communication needs* of the child, and in the case of a child who is *deaf or hard of hearing,* consider the child's language and communication needs, opportunities for direct communications with peers and professional personnel in the child's language and communication mode, academic level, and full range of needs, including opportunities for direct instruction in the child's language and communication mode; and

(v) Consider whether the child needs *assistive technology* devices and services.

Key: IDEA, Individuals with Disabilities Education Improvement Act; IEP, individualized education program

Source: From U.S. Department of Education. (2012). Individuals with Disabilities Education Act, 34 C.F.R. §300.324(a)(2)(i)-(v).

- Specific social skills

- The ability to communicate effectively across educational settings

- Nonverbal social skills

- Self-management skills and emotion regulation

- Self-advocacy, self-esteem, and self-determination skills

In addition, the team should ensure the student understands and masters the skills for reporting bullying to an adult. The student may require one-to-one instructions to learn the steps for identifying and reporting bullying to an adult. Other modifications and accommodations may include preferential seating on the bus, counseling services, increased supervision, related services (e.g., speech and language therapy), and regularly scheduled meetings with team members to ensure consistent implementation and protections from harassment.

 Don't allow people to degrade you and attempt to make you feel inferior. Being different from the norm is acceptable. I can't stress enough that you need to love yourself. Seek help from a school counselor or teacher.

TRAINING FOR STUDENTS WITH DISABILITIES

The IEP or 504 plan for students who are victims of bullying should address the skills needed to avoid and respond appropriately to a bullying incident. If a student with disabilities is getting bullied on the bus, the written plan should identify specific goals to teach the student age-appropriate behaviors for avoiding bullying situations (e.g., sit in the front seat), addressing the bully with an effective response, and reporting bullying to an adult. In this example, the education team provides multiple opportunities for proactively teaching skills in order to maintain the student's related services before restricting the student's transportation to a specialized bus. Although changing school buses may be deemed appropriate in the short term, it ultimately restricts the student's opportunity to socialize with peers and stigmatizes the student who will be noticeably riding a different bus from his or her peers in the neighborhood. The IEP and 504 plan is written to teach students appropriate replacement skills to access the general education setting.

Teaching students with disabilities to prevent or respond to an incident of bullying or disability-based harassment must encompass clear, simple, and concrete skills repeatedly taught in a variety of settings. As discussed, the Stop-Walk-Talk (Ross, Horner, & Stiller, 2008) approach is a simple three-step protocol for teaching students how to respond to an incident of bullying and reporting to an

adult. A similar protocol should be used when teaching students with disabilities the appropriate skills for preventing or responding to a bullying attempt.
Dr. Michelle Borba has designed an anti-bullying protocol for typically developing students that can be adapted and taught to students with disabilities:

 http://www.micheleborba.com

The CALM approach describes plainly how a student should respond to a
bully. Here are the steps for the CALM approach:

Cool down: The first step for responding to a bully is to "cool down" or remain
    calm. Teach students to recognize stress signals and learn calming strategies.
    Deep breathing and positive value statements are practiced with students of
    any age. For schools that have adopted a social-emotional learning (SEL) cur-
    riculum, the skills for self-management, self-control, and self-regulation can
    be adapted for students with disabilities. Self-soothing helps children calm
    down by using messages, affirmations, or visual imagery (Craig, 2008).

Assert yourself: Part of a comprehensive social skills curriculum for students
    with disabilities includes teaching assertive body language. Role-playing
    and video modeling can assist in teaching nonverbal body language that
    can deflect and detour bullying attempts. Students are shown appropriate
    nonverbal skills for standing tall with their head up and shoulders squared
    when moving through the school or responding to a bully.

Look them in the eye: Although eye contact can be difficult for some students
    with disabilities, school professionals should teach students how to face
    bullies and look them in the eye. Visual supports and social narratives
    (described later) are beneficial for teaching students how to utilize eye
    contact during a bullying incident. Provide options or accommodations for
    students with physical disabilities or visual impairments.

Mean it: Self-advocacy skills and communication skills are important when
    addressing and responding to a bully. A speech and language therapist, along
    with parent support, should work directly with the victim of bullying on spe-
    cific language scripts for how to respond to a bully. Teach a nonconfronta-
    tional script such as "Stop that," "Leave me alone," "You are being a bully," or
    "Get away from me now." According to a recent research study by Davis and
    Nixon (2014), students reported that the most helpful self-action they could
    take when responding to bullying was to "make a joke about it." Teachers
    and therapists can consider age-appropriate jokes and humor as a way to
    deflect hostilities without recommending disparaging remarks or hurtful

responses. For students with communication or language impairments, a simple appropriate gesture and response may suffice when responding to a bully.

The CALM approach is just one example of a response protocol that provides an easy-to-remember framework for teaching students the steps for responding to a bully. Students that are effectively taught these steps with multiple opportunities for practice are provided a level of protection from incidents of harassment.

 Walk with your head held high, tell yourself everyday "I will do something great today," and focus on what makes you feel good. You need to feel confident in who you are and not try to mold yourself into someone you can't be. Your life is worthwhile. You have to take what you have and make yourself feel big. It may be hard, but high school is only for 4 years and you have the rest of your life. Stay close to your family and friends.

It is important for school personnel to select evidence-based practices for teaching students with disabilities to respond to bullying and harassment. The education team should review and select a variety of instructional methods for teaching students the necessary prosocial skills. The following are structured teaching methods to help students develop skills to prevent bullying and harassment:

1. *Video modeling:* Video modeling is a mode of teaching that involves the student watching appropriate verbal and nonverbal interactions on video and imitating the behavior of the model. The idea behind video modeling is to teach the student to imitate a sequence of positive and successful social-communication skills such as initiating play, offering to help, playing a game, or having lunch in the cafeteria (Nikopoulos & Keenan, 2006). Video modeling has been shown to be an evidence-based method for teaching students with ASD (Franzone & Collet-Klingenberg, 2008; NAC, 2009). For more detailed information, refer to *How to Use Video Modeling and Video Prompting* (Sigafoos, O'Reilly, & de la Cruz, 2007).

2. *Role playing and drama:* Instruct students to practice, dramatize, act, and demonstrate social-communication skills in a controlled small group. School counselors, school psychologists, and other school personnel can conduct small groups that engage students in role-playing self-advocacy skills, assertiveness, and conflict resolution. Create rule-governed scenarios that occur throughout the school day and have students portray the scenes and practice nonverbal skills. Interactive role playing can provide multiple examples of social situations that can arise in school. Peers can

be taught to interact appropriately during a role-playing skit. Videotaping the sessions provides an opportunity for viewing and dissecting the scenes in slow motion or pausing a scene to identify the nonverbal skills.

3. *Scripting:* Provide students with short and concise scripts (one or two sentences) of what to say and how to behave in social situations. Scripting is a story-based intervention and involves written information that is designed to teach social-communication skills (NAC, 2009). Scripting teaches critical information such as the essential components of a conversation: initial introduction, descriptive details on topic, and ending a conversation. Scripting builds on language the student has mastered and then expands to other topics (Ganz, 2007). Topics include how to ask for help, saying hello to a friend, asking what you did last night, and what to say if you are being bullied. The script should include age-appropriate vocabulary and visual supports, which will teach students what to say and how to say it in different scenarios.

4. *Social narratives:* Social narratives, like scripting, are based on written materials presented to the student to describe social scenarios and appropriate responses (Collett-Klingenberg & Franzone, 2008). Social narratives, or Social Stories, were first developed by Carol Gray (1995). This method utilizes clear and concise sentences and highlights with visual icons and symbols to direct student behavior. Social narratives incorporate age-appropriate words and pictures to detail common contingencies of how to respond in a variety of settings. Social narratives allow for repetition, as they are readily available and accessible to review repeatedly. Some social narratives can be recycled and used for many topics and situations, such as "How do I start a game of soccer at recess?"; "What do I say when someone insults me?"; and "How should I respond to a bully?" The general point is that social narratives provide students with easy access to clear descriptions of social situations and concrete responses of appropriate behaviors (see Appendix D for sample scripts).

5. *Self-management:* Promoting independence through self-management or self-monitoring is an important lifelong skill. Self-monitoring is the personal application of social-emotional skills or communication skills or the steps to bullying prevention that are being targeted for mastery—this includes identifying behaviors that are targeted for bullying (Rose & Monda-Amaya, 2011). Students are taught to record their own behaviors and incorporate a self-assessment in the process and to discriminate between appropriate and inappropriate behaviors during a conflict or bullying incident. Students with disabilities are provided with a checklist to determine if they followed the steps for the CALM approach or similar steps for responding appropriately and effectively to a bullying incident or conflicts with peers. This type of self-management increases student accountability and is tied to the reinforcement schedule whereby students

receive reinforcement for evaluating their behaviors. Adult supervision and feedback is necessary when first teaching new skills and then faded over time. Self-monitoring promotes independence and lifelong learning and awareness of social-communication skills and is an evidence-based practice according to the National Professional Development Center (Neitzel & Busick, 2009).

Students who master skills for initiating a social interaction, maintaining personal space, and displaying appropriate nonverbal behaviors are less likely to be victimized by bullies and more likely to be supported by empathetic peers. Therefore, it is essential that educators explicitly teach students the necessary skills to appropriately respond during a bullying incident and to stop bullying when possible.

In addition to identifying and teaching specific skills for bullying prevention, self-advocacy and self-determination support a student's strengths. Self-confidence and feelings of self-worth are important antidotes to ongoing bullying and the long-term ill effects of harassment. Focusing on goal setting, self awareness, and strengths empowers students and can minimize the effects of bullying and harassment (Rose & Monda-Amaya, 2011). The education team, along with the student, should carefully consider the strengths of the student and develop a plan to identify and incorporate interests, hobbies, and activities where the student can demonstrate age-appropriate skills. According to Ragozzino and Utne-O'brien (2009), all students should be given opportunities to be valued and respected in the classroom and opportunities to foster a sense of self-worth. Community-based activities or volunteer opportunities provide experiences to build self-esteem by giving back to the community. For example, a mother shared that her 17-year-old daughter with ASD was tutoring younger students in math during an after-school program. Her daughter excelled in math in elementary school and loved working with children. This activity greatly increased her self-confidence and helped minimize some of the difficulties she was experiencing with her teenage peers and social exclusion.

When teaching new skills to students, the education team should incorporate reinforcement strategies as the student masters new skills. Some students with disabilities will not be intrinsically reinforced to follow the steps of a concrete response protocol (e.g., the CALM approach), whereas other students may require more direct and tangible reinforcers such as a favorite toy or object, food or snack, or activity (e.g., computer time). Therefore, the education team should carefully assess students for potential reinforcers and determine a reinforcement schedule for acquiring and maintaining new skills. Reinforcers do not have to be extravagant or require much instructional time or planning. For example, extra free time, a homework pass, being the first in line for the day, being named student of the week, or picking a book to read are easily implemented for students of any age. The education team must develop potential reinforcers while taking observable data for progress monitoring to ensure students are mastering newly taught skills.

I know that your parents care for you deeply. And they want nothing but the best for you. Please tell an adult about the other kids being mean to you. Confronting the problem is the best way to make it go away. Growing up can be tough but it's worth it. I hope this helps to give you hope.

Implementation Checklist

Can you . . . ?   **Yes**

Define the bystander effect   ☐

Develop a bystander response protocol   ☐

Identify various peer responses for an incident of bullying   ☐

List the benefits of peer mentoring   ☐

Describe the factors that may contribute to increased bullying behaviors
   in schools   ☐

Brainstorm graduated consequences for bullying   ☐

Convey to all staff the need to address bullying in a student's
   individualized education program (IEP) or 504 plan   ☐

Prepare lesson plans to teach the CALM approach   ☐

Report

Talk to your school principal. Tell her to stop bullying in your school. Talk to her about the dangers of bullying and that many kids get hurt. Einstein once said, "The world is a bad place. Not because of the evil people in it, but because of the people who do nothing about it." You, my friend, have the courage to speak out as I have already seen. This is your life, your moment, your time.

Results-Driven Accountability

I n order to reduce victimization and protect students from harmful bullying and harassment before it begins, school personnel must carefully measure and analyze both qualitative and quantitative data to ensure the safety of all students. School district superintendents and administrators, along with teachers and parents, must be transparent in how they will effectively measure the incidence of bullying in each school and direct resources to guard against disability-based harassment. Bullying and harassment laws, policies, interventions, and activities are meaningless unless each school identifies and defines the parameters for ongoing assessment for results-driven accountability. The U.S. Department of Education states, "Collecting and analyzing data on bullying behaviors can provide a clearer picture of what is happening in schools and school activities, guide planning or prevention, instruction, and intervention efforts over time" (2013, p. 5).

Unfortunately, data collection around the incidence of bullying in schools is scarce. There is a significant gap between the national prevalence rates of bullying and the number of locally reported cases of bullying to teachers, school leaders, or state educational agencies. Most schools lack sufficient data of the occurrence and effects of bullying at the individual school level (U.S. Department of Education, 2011). Less than half of U.S. states have written policies that require publicly reporting bullying incidence rates, and only 10 states require that school district employees formally report bullying (Swearer, Espelage, & Napolitano, 2009). Adding to this lack of quantitative data, school personnel have difficulty estimating and detecting incidents of bullying and harassment. According to the American Educational Research Association (AERA; 2013), "Adults often report that school safety is a mild or moderate problem, while students within the same school often report that it is a severe problem" (p. 37). Adding to this complex issue of underestimating rates of bullying by teachers, only 25%–50% of students tell school personnel about an incident of bullying (Strohmeier & Noam, 2012). Without formal reporting measures, there is a dramatic chasm between the well-established national prevalence rates of bullying in schools and the local school district reporting data.

"Bullying Incidents Low in Local School District"

A recent headline in an online article posted from a small school district in the southern United States reported only 17 cases of bullying for the entire student population of 1,471 students (Richardson, 2014). Using the national prevalence rates for calculating bullying would estimate approximately 411 reports of bullying, or 28% of the student population (Robers et al., 2012). Unfortunately, the superintendent reported to the school board less than 2% of students were bullied, and of the 17 reported cases, only 9 qualified as a bullying violation. This level of underestimating bullying in schools is a nationwide problem.

As demonstrated by this article, a dramatic chasm exists between student reporting of bullying to the school and the currently accepted prevalence rates of bullying and harassment in any given school. This puts the onus on school leaders to collect data from multiple sources to confirm actual rates of bullying. Preventing bullying and harassment requires consistent and reliable assessment tools and regular data collection that focuses on a range of safety-related issues throughout the school year to guide educational programming. School leaders and teachers must set high, measurable standards for student safety and protecting students from harassment. The school's adopted technical assistance guide (TAG) should include quantifiable goals for reducing rates of bullying and harassment based on current school data. For example, if the baseline assessment data confirms that bullying is affecting 23% of the student population of 500 students, or 115 students, then the school safety team (SST) can write a measurable goal to reduce bullying rates by 20% to 92 students in the initial phases of implementing a prevention program. Interventions and activities are then designed to meet the schoolwide measurable goal.

Prevalence versus Incidence Rates

Prevalence is the proportion of the population, such as a school, that may be affected or at risk for bullying or harassment. These are typically percentages from large surveys or group studies. Incidence rates, however, are the actual number of new cases of bullying affecting students at a particular school at any point in time. The average prevalence rates are reported at 28% for students 12–18 years of age (Robers et al., 2012), but any given school may have a smaller incidence rate due to effective intervention practices or due to ineffective reporting measures.

Don't let these ignorant kids control your life, you are the master of your life, do positive things with it. Your strength is inevitable and will shine on others. You have inspired me, never give up, your future is bright. It is possible to create the perfect life, and soon enough it will come to you.

ASSESSMENT DATA

Results-driven accountability and data-based decision making is a key feature for implementation and sustainability of bullying prevention programs. As previously mentioned, most schools have a written vision or mission statement that generally contains two essential tenets:

1. Foster a positive school climate and create a safe learning environment for all students.

2. Focus on academic achievement and high educational standards.

Student academic achievement is measured with a multitude of reliable measures: standardized tests, graduation rates, performance interim assessments, dropout rates, attendance, retention rates, and a variety of grade-level achievement tests. Unfortunately, there is a scarcity of valid and reliable assessment for school climate or rates of student victimization, including a lack of reporting measures for incidence rates of bullying. This is a roadblock to accountability and student outcomes. Here are some possible questions for baseline data collection:

- How are school leaders and teachers evaluating a respectful environment where all students feel connected?

- Are school personnel measuring kindness, fairness, equity, and student-teacher relationships?

- Do students have a fear of being bullied? How do bystanders react to bullying?

- How are individual schools assessing the incidence rates of bullying and harassment?

- How many incidents of bullying were reported last year? Compare data from last year to the current year.

Without a variety of valid assessment tools, school personnel are uninformed and not held accountable for student outcomes. A lack of quantifiable data can create a real sense of denial that bullying and harassment is a current problem in school. For example, a principal at an educational seminar remarked that his school did not have a bullying problem. Although the school district never collected bullying data, the principal "just knew that they were good kids from good families. Moreover, if there were a problem, I would know about it." What this school leader—and every courageous school leader—needs to do is gather multiple forms of data to confirm the rates of bullying. School leaders must be transparent in collecting, analyzing, and implementing data-based decision making. Then and only then will they be able to say with confidence whether they have a bullying problem in their school.

Preventing and reducing the rates of bullying and harassment must be regularly measured and embedded as part of the broader school safety plan. Schools routinely collect data for guns in schools, theft, battery, aggression or fighting, and other safety issues. These same standards must be applied to bullying and harassment data.

SCHOOL SURVEYS

School leaders, members of the SST, and experts in assessment and evaluation procedures must work collaboratively to create and implement accurate data collection tools that target bullying and harassment. The tools and assessment measures should focus on the local school districts' and individual school's rate and type of bullying. The school survey is one type of measurement tool used for collecting data efficiently for future planning of multitiered interventions. A school survey can provide data on the broader school climate but also digs deeper into the data surrounding specific types of bullying and harassment.

If school leaders restrict data analysis to only reporting statistics, the overall need for intensive interventions, services, and resources will be underestimated. As mentioned earlier, only a small percentage of students report bullying to adults and often bullying goes undetected by school personnel (Bradshaw, Sawyer, & O'Brennan, 2007). This is not meant to place the blame or fault on teachers; some types of bullying are difficult to detect. Relational bullying, social exclusion, and cyberbullying are not easily observed. Therefore, school personnel and the SST must develop and implement alternate data collection methods such as a school surveys for students, staff, and parents. An anonymous school survey is the benchmark for any bullying and harassment prevention program. Not only are surveys recommended by the U.S. Department of Education (2013); the overwhelming consensus from research-based programs such as the Olweus Bullying Prevention Program (OBPP) and Second Steps begins with a baseline needs assessment or surveys to collect data and identify the school's current needs.

 Try to surround yourself with peers who are optimistic and respectful. Don't let their rudeness bother you so much, they are not worth it. Don't waste your time thinking of them. They are tormenting an innocent, lovely person like you. Being unique is a blessing, not a shame. Don't conform and think outside the box.

Surveys are appropriate to track the effectiveness for each component of a bullying prevention program. For example, preintervention and postintervention surveys are conducted to compare different intervention strategies. For example, baseline survey questions might ask students to state the rules for effectively responding to an incident of bullying. After implementing a bystander protocol and intensive training, the school can conduct a postintervention survey and analyze the different responses from students (Table 7.1). Surveys help target specific interventions and assist the SST in assessing and prioritizing the core components for a comprehensive multitiered program.

Assessment tools for measuring school climate are not as readily available or marketed to schools as standardized academic tests. Fortunately, the Centers for Disease Control and Prevention (CDC) have published two important documents to assist educators in creating and measuring school climate and bullying in schools. These free online resources allow the SST and others to individualize a measurement tool or survey or adopt an already published assessment tool:

1. *Measuring Bullying Victimization, Perpetration, and Bystander Experiences: A Compendium of Assessment Tools* (Hamburger, Basile, & Vivolo, 2011).

   This document provides educators with a variety of assessment tools that have been designed to measure a range of school experiences that include 33 measures and scales written between 1990 and 2007. This compendium represents a starting point from which educators can consider a set of psychometrically sound measures for assessing self-reported incidence and prevalence of a variety of bullying experiences. The range of measures includes aggression scales, victimization scales, teasing scales, cyberbullying surveys, and bystander scales. All of the measures have been published in peer-reviewed journals. Some of the measurement tools are copyright protected and may require publisher permission for use in schools. The SST may utilize this document and select appropriate assessment tools as a template or framework for creating a school survey to investigate the incidence of bullying and harassment. For more information, visit the CDC web site:

   http://www.cdc.gov/violenceprevention/pub/measuring_bullying.html

Table 7.1.　Preintervention and postintervention results

Preintervention results	Postintervention results
39% of students could identify the three-step Stop-Walk-Talk protocol for responding to an incident of bullying.	93% of students could identify the three-step protocol for responding to an incident of bullying.

2. *Bullying Surveillance Among Youths: Uniform Definitions for Public Health and Recommended Data Elements* (Gladden et al., 2014).

This document provides a uniform definition of bullying as well as the core data elements utilized in creating high-quality surveys and assessment tools. Not only does this document provide the core elements for a survey; it also identifies expanded data types to increase the scope of a survey to capture the bullying experience and prevalence of bullying in school. This document is invaluable for assisting the SST in writing and developing surveys that measure rates of not only bullying but also disability harassment. This document provides sample questions and measurement guidelines. The document contains a thorough description for each data point, uses in schools, coding instructions, and other citations and references that would be helpful to the SST in writing a school survey. For more information, visit the CDC web site:

http://www.cdc.gov/violenceprevention/pdf/bullying-definitions-final-a.pdf

The SST and other school personnel should review these existing surveys and modify them for the individual school. School surveys are part of the school's technical assistance guide (TAG) and disseminated to all schools.

In addition to the CDC recommendations, a variety of school surveys are available online from various state educational agencies. For example, Colorado, California, and New Jersey have written online school climate surveys that may be adapted by other state or local educational agencies. The Colorado Trust, created and published the Bullying Prevention Initiative, offers a downloadable survey for staff and students:

http://www.coloradotrust.org/attachments/0002/1691/BPI_Student_Survey _no-copyright.pdf

Many of these surveys can be easily modified to meet the unique needs of the school and students across grade levels and developmental needs (Table 7.2).

It is not enough to design a survey with only general questions regarding school climate; a school survey designed for reducing bullying must dig deeper into the specifics of bullying and harassment. For example, the California

Table 7.2.   Key features for school surveys

1. Supportive school environments, including the physical environment

2. Caring and trusted staff who focus on how people treat each other

3. Meaningful student participation and an environment where students feel included

4. An environment where equity and diversity are respected and valued

5. School connectedness, sense of belonging, and collegiality

Healthy Kids Survey (n.d.) asks students to reply yes or no to statements related to bullying prevention in order to gain their honest and anonymous responses:

- Teachers here make it clear to students that bullying is not tolerated.

- If another student was bullying me, I would tell one of the teachers or staff at school.

- Students tell teachers when other students are being bullied.

- If I tell a teacher that someone is bullying me, the teacher will do something to help.

- Students here try to stop bullying when they see it happening.

Bullying Surveillance Among Youths (Gladden et al., 2014) suggests expanding school surveys to yield additional information and probe deeper into the context and description of bullying incidents:

1. Were there witnesses to bullying (bystanders), and how many adults were present?

2. Did the victim tell an adult, and did the adult take action?

3. How many perpetrators were there—one or more?

4. What was the level of harm experienced by the victim?

5. Did the incident involve free or reduced lunch recipients?

6. Did the victim have health problems such as obesity, diabetes, asthma, or allergies?

The purpose of these expanded questions assists the SST in not only understanding the demographics of bullies and victims but tracking additional factors such as how school staff or peers support students who are victims of bullying or harassment. Expanded questions inquire about the number of students or adults who directly intervened to stop the bullying. Expanded questions probe attitudes, opinions, and other issues that may contribute to a thorough understanding of bullying and harassment. This expanded data can be tracked separately and measured over time to analyze for trends. One trend that should be analyzed by the SST is the frequency and intensity of adult intervention during a bullying incident.

> ### Sample Survey Questions
>
> *Adults will intervene to stop bullying:*
>   0—Rarely; 1—Sometimes; 2—Often; 3—Always
>
> *I am bullied at home:*
>   0—Rarely; 1—Sometimes; 2—Often; 3—Always
>
> *Bullying at school makes it difficult to learn:*
>   0—Rarely; 1—Sometimes; 2—Often; 3—Always

Surveys can be designed to measure a variety of data points and issues surrounding general school safety, positive school climate, and bullying. Some surveys, such as the California Healthy Kids Survey, ask simple yes or no questions. Other surveys utilize a Likert scale (1 for "never" to 5 for "always"). Surveys may also include open-ended questions that ask the student to describe a bullying incident or other descriptive sentences and opinions, such as "How did teachers respond to the incident?" SurveyMonkey.com has partnered with the U.S. Department of Education to create a series of bullying survey templates, available here:

 https://www.surveymonkey.com/blog/en/bullying-survey-template/

A word of caution—it is important that students with disabilities have access to all written documents and surveys. The SST must consider a student's disability and make modifications to schoolwide surveys (e.g., braille, voice output devices, surveys read orally). Due to the high rates of victimization, students with disabilities must be provided multiple opportunities to share experiences and identify any concerns. All students require adequate and effective training to understand the terminology and language utilized in an anonymous survey. If the SST has not adopted and implemented bystander awareness and education protocols, then students will have difficulty describing the level of bystander involvement, as they may not understand the concept. They may not even know the vocabulary or label for a bystander. Also, if classroom teachers have not effectively and repeatedly taught the difference between normal childhood conflict and bullying, students may overrate bullying in the affirmative when asked, "Have you witnessed bullying at school?" Developing and administering valid surveys requires time and skills for writing a reliable measurement tool that provides school personnel and parents with transparent objective data in order to meet the needs of the students.

First of all, I am sorry you are bullied. It happens to all of us. Tell your parents. Your parents may help you out. Maybe you can switch math class, teachers should not yell at you. I am not very good at math either. Well, that is all my advice. A friend.

Students are not the only group that should be surveyed. Parents and staff should also have multiple opportunities to identify and provide input on the school's strengths and areas for improvement. A staff survey might ask questions regarding the social validity of, value of, and student satisfaction with the current bullying prevention program. These questions can include the following:

- How well do you understand the bullying prevention program at our school?

- How effective is the school's bystander education program?

- How well do you feel supported in implementing a multitiered evidence-based bullying prevention program?

- Do you need further training? What type of training—in print or online professional development?

In order to identify and plan for future changes to the multitiered bullying prevention program, the SST must collect data from a variety of sources. For example, an anonymous survey from ancillary support staff such as custodians, office assistants, and cafeteria personnel provides unique data as to the prevalence of bullying in hot spots. As with most recommendations for preventing bullying and harassment (e.g., bystander education), school surveys do not pose a funding issue, as they do not require additional funding and only very little instructional time, but they do require a high level of professional commitment to school improvement and student safety.

It may not be feasible or efficient to survey all students as to their level of knowledge of school rules about bullying or the adopted bystander protocols for responding to a bullying incident. Another option for information gathering comes from random surveys or a sampling of students. The SST may create shorter surveys and other more efficient options for periodically monitoring bullying throughout the school year. For example, randomly survey 10%–15% of the student body to ask targeted questions on the nature of bullying, general school safety, and school procedures for reporting. Randomized surveys and probes should be conducted periodically throughout the school year to avoid delaying results to the end of the school year. The SST should determine the acceptable criteria for each response. For example, perhaps the goal is for 80%–85% of randomly selected students to be able to state the school policy on bullying, identify the action steps for being a bystander, and identify how to report a bullying incident. Information collected by the SST is reviewed for trends to guide and prioritize intervention practices during the school year.

While the SST and schoolwide surveys are conducted mainly as summative assessments by comparing pre- and postsurvey scores for trends at the end of the school year, classroom teachers can create shorter versions of the school survey that target specific skills for students at the classroom level as a formative or interim assessment. The classroom teacher can quickly assess the results of a survey to reflect on instructional practices and aid in guiding future lesson plans on bullying prevention or social-emotional learning (SEL). For example, do students know the steps or rules for the bystander protocol? Can students identify the steps for reporting a bullying incident? These classroom-level surveys should be anonymous and used for instructional planning. "Data-driven instruction practices succeed only when it is truly teacher-owned, meaning teachers must personally analyze their own classes' data" (Bambrick-Santoyo, 2010, p. xxxi). Therefore, the end-of-the-year school report that summarizes the total number of bullying incidents within an entire school will not benefit the classroom teacher in making immediate effective data-based decisions in the classroom. Short, periodic classroom surveys assist educators in tracking progress and maintaining a safe, positive educational environment.

FOCUS GROUPS

Schoolwide anonymous surveys are just one form of data collection or overall assessment in schools. Conducting and facilitating focus groups is an effective means to collect pertinent information on topics of school safety and bullying. Focus groups can be used to gather multiple perspectives and opinions about school climate and the incidence of bullying (AERA, 2013). Focus groups promote dialogue among parents, students, and other represented stakeholders. The school principal or SST can facilitate a guided discussion on issues of school safety and bullying. The group may consist of a targeted group of parents of children with disabilities and other protected classes. Not only do focus groups generate keen insight; they can be essential in creating a positive, caring climate by seeking input and ideas about specific interventions. For example, the groups may be asked to discuss the strengths and weaknesses of the school's web site and the tips for parents on bullying prevention. Focus groups are an excellent solution to public relations with parents and another way to fulfill the obligations and recommendations from Epstein's framework of six types of parental involvement (Chapter 4).

Focus groups are an effective means for periodically soliciting student and family input regarding the school community. Focus groups assist school leaders to acquire additional information to inform the implementation of new proposals or programs. A student focus group may be asked to review a new peer mentoring program or schoolwide assembly. The students share opinions and comments on how to improve student-directed programs. Student responses are recorded, or someone from the SST is assigned to take notes and highlight responses. A written record of the focus group meeting is reviewed and analyzed for consistent recurring themes. An executive summary of the focus group meeting is written to including findings and conclusions. This document can be utilized to create baseline data at the initial planning stages for a bullying prevention program or throughout the school year to determine immediate needs of the school plan. The findings from a focus group meeting are also included as part of the annual yearly report for revising policies and procedures within the continuous school improvement plan.

Implementation Checklist

Can you . . . ?   **Yes**

Identify the purpose for collecting baseline data   ☐

Respond to the national prevalence rates of data but the lack of local
    data collection   ☐

Explain the difference between prevalence rates and incidence rates   ☐

Design a student survey that focuses on bullying and harassment   ☐

Plan a focus group for students with disabilities   ☐

Bullying and Harassment
Reports and Investigation Procedures

Surveys and focus groups provide critical information for assessing and developing a comprehensive multitiered prevention program, but school leaders and the school safety team (SST) must also collect data surrounding every incident of bullying or harassment. A written reporting form is central to informing policy and future planning as well as holding schools accountable for rates of bullying and harassment. A written form provides school leaders with the relevant information to effectively investigate and ensure the protections necessary for students with disabilities. The reporting form is part of the adopted school policy and procedures and includes standardized information. The U.S. Department of Education disseminated a Dear Colleague Letter (DCL) titled "Anti-Bullying Policies: Examples of Provisions in State Laws" (2010) to "serve as technical assistance for those stakeholders looking to develop or revise anti-bullying legislation or policies." They identified 11 key components for developing and implementing anti-bullying legislation, citing examples from various state laws (Table 8.1).

The U.S. Department of Education advises local educational agencies to create reporting procedures for incidents of bullying. Specifically, the U.S. Department of Education DCL (2010) recommends the following:

> Students, students' families, staff, and others can report incidents of bullying, including a process to submit such information anonymously and with protection from retaliation. The procedure identifies and provides contact information for the appropriate school personnel responsible for receiving the report and investigating the incident. (p. 4)

According to the U.S. Department of Education's *Analysis of State Bullying Laws and Policies* (2011), 24 states do not have any requirements for staff or students to

Table 8.1.   Key components in state anti-bullying laws

1. Purpose statement

2. Statement of scope

3. Specification of prohibited conduct

4. Enumeration of specific characteristics

5. Development and implementation of local educational agencies' (LEAs') policies

6. Components of LEA policies

7. Review of local policies

8. Communication plan

9. Training and preventive education

10. Transparency and monitoring

11. Statement of rights to other legal recourse

Source: From U.S. Department of Health and Human Services. (2014). Key components in state anti-bullying laws. Retrieved from http://www.stopbullying.gov/laws/key-components

report bullying, whereas 15 states require all school staff to report bullying and 2 states require both staff and students to report bullying. Wisconsin state law and policies require staff to report bullying:

> 118.46.1(a) (2009): "The [policy on bullying] shall include all of the following: . . . (6) A requirement that school district officials and employees report incidents of bullying and identify the persons to whom the reports must be made."

Washington State's model policy requires that "any school staff who observes, overhears, or otherwise witnesses bullying or harassment, must take immediate appropriate action and report it promptly" (Washington State Office of the Education Ombudsman, 2011). Clearly, the research and guidance from the federal and state level suggests all school-district employees should formally report incidents of bullying and harassment, regardless if they directly witness a bullying incident or have been indirectly told by others. Without standard reporting procedures, school leaders and the SST will be ineffective in protecting students from bullying and disability-based harassment and future planning of evidence-based interventions. In order to meet this goal, the SST and school leaders must create a reporting form.

 Communication is key; tell your teachers or the principal. I write music to help me cope. I can release my emotions and it keeps me happy. As you grow older, bullying will end with maturity. You are better than those kids, and I respect your strength.

THE BULLYING AND HARASSMENT REPORT FORM

The bullying and harassment report form is critical for addressing and measuring school safety and bullying. Without quantitative reporting data, it would be very easy to deny the rate of bullying in a school and disregard the need for future improvement plans for prevention. School leaders must be held accountable for rates of bullying, with a focus on data-based decision making. Here are some considerations for school leaders along with key stakeholders for creating a bullying and harassment report form (Appendix E):

1. Create a specific bullying and harassment report form and avoid using a generic "incident" form to track cases of bullying and harassment. With numerous school policies and regulations, there are many educational documents and forms within a school district. An "incident report form," a "nurse's report form," a "discipline form," or the "bus incident form" is too generic. An incident report form covers issues from student violence, substance abuse, criminal mischief, vandalism, or weapons in school. This type of reporting form is not conducive for tracking and monitoring different types of bullying and harassment because it does not disaggregate the data by type of bullying. In addition, a general school incident form may not trigger the necessary steps for an investigation as required by federal and state laws for bullying and disability-based harassment.

2. Encompass standardized data such as the date and type of bullying or harassment and identify the source (e.g., staff, parent, student, self-report). The Centers for Disease Control and Prevention (CDC; 2014) has identified core elements to be included for all data collection systems in order to track the magnitude, scope, and characteristics of bullying and harassment. The core elements on a bullying report form should include the source (name optional); time period; frequency; type of bullying; location; grade level; staff members involved; witnesses; and demographic information such as disability status, sex, race, grade level, English proficiency, religion, and sexual orientation. The report form should include a designation for involvement of a student with a disability. School leaders along with the SST should review state or district model policies to ensure the form has all required components (e.g., disclosures, legal language) and can be easily tracked and analyzed for future planning.

3. Assign a case number to identify the incident and avoid duplication from multiple sources. For example, a teacher may write a report of a bullying incident he or she observed in the courtyard, whereas a bystander may file an anonymous report online regarding the same incident and a parent may have phoned the school administrator with the additional details. Each file is assigned to the same confidential case number in order to track each incident of bullying and gather all facts. It may be helpful to cross-reference student identification numbers with the bullying incident ID number for the purposes of not only analyzing the data by the number of incidents but also tracking specific students who have been involved with situations of bullying or harassment (e.g., victim-bully) to investigate necessary supports.

4. Promote accessibility for reporting. Reporting methods should be simple and disseminated to all students, parents, and staff. All reporting forms must be accessible to students with disabilities (e.g., braille). The SST may need to consider accommodations for submitting a report form, such as having them available to students with physical disabilities. Sample documents may be sent home at the beginning of the school year or made available in classrooms and central locations.

5. Establish multiple methods for reporting, including a formal school-district-generated document (a bully and harassment report form) and also web-based anonymous reports, phone hot line to school, or other digital means such as text-based reporting by phone. As more schools are utilizing technology in the classrooms, review options of reporting through smartphones by text message or newly developed bullying apps (e.g., Bully Alert). Traditional methods of paper documents or report forms may be disseminated throughout the school in student-populated areas (cafeteria, entranceway). Schools can place locked boxes in central locations for anonymous reporting and disseminate information as to how often the box is checked. This free and simple idea not only provides an avenue for students to report; it also sends a visual message that school leaders are inviting students to participate in creating safe schools. For example, a program called Hero in the Hallway urges bystanders to report bullying and reminds helpful bystanders that they can be effective in decreasing victimization:

 http://www.herointhehallway.com

6. Require staff to respond to all reports of bullying. If the school's bystander education protocol instructs students to report to an adult, then school leaders must ensure that all staff are receptive and take action when a student comes forward to report a bullying incident. If students are repeatedly advised to report to an adult if someone is in trouble but the teacher does not take action or consistently minimizes the student's concerns, then students will quickly learn from their adult role models that bullying is not taken seriously. Programs such as Expect Respect (Stiller, Nese, Tomlanovich, Horner, & Ross, 2013) not only focus on training the students to be responsible for reporting but also include teacher and staff coaching on how to appropriately respond when a student reports. Adults must respond with supportive statements to let students know they have been heard and to guide them toward effective action steps. The Expect

Respect handbook includes a staff self-assessment titled "Fidelity Checklist for Staff Members," with questions such as "To what extent have I praised the student for reporting the bullying and harassment incident?" (p. 58). A fidelity checklist reminds all staff of the importance of implementation and staff responsibility to adequately respond.

I understand what it is like to be bullied for your interests. I am 16 and have had to make more changes for myself. I have told teachers about getting bullied and it backfired. So I won't give you that advice. It just made it worse and nothing was done. Now I embrace myself to the fullest extent possible and as a result, others have followed suit. I wish you the best in life.

Reporting Adult Mistreatment

When developing reporting methods, it is important to remember that adult mistreatment to a student may also be reported. Adults with supervisory control over students may exhibit behaviors that are seen as abusive or create a hostile environment. Most school policies do not address this issue, and students may fear retaliation for reporting an incident to a teacher or other staff member. School policies should make clear that all students and staff are required to demonstrate respectful behavior and adult mistreatment of students will not be tolerated (McEvoy, 2005).

---

7. Provide concrete examples and training for writing and describing an incident of bullying. Examples may include the rules and consequences for false reporting. It should be noted that the research does not suggest that if schools provide students with opportunities to report bullying, then this will increase false reporting. If school leaders and the SST are concerned about false reporting, it is suggested they include a statement in the policy and student code of conduct, educate students about the consequences of false reporting, and consistently follow through with any individual cases that have been reported falsely. For example, a school district in Florida includes the following statement in the school policy:

> False accusations or reports of bullying or harassment against another student are prohibited. A person who engages in false reporting of bullying and harassment shall be subject to discipline for that act in accordance with school board policies.

School leaders should promote any and all reporting and not limit access based on false accusations. According to an anonymous middle school assistant principal, "There's never too much information when it comes to helping a student with a social issue."

8. Designate a school official (e.g., anti-bullying coordinator) assigned to receive, gather, or collect bullying report forms or online reports. School policies should publicly identify the staff member who ultimately receives all written reports, and students and parents should be made aware of the school official designee. The written policy may identify this position by title (e.g., school counselor) or responsibility within the school (e.g., dean of students) and be clearly posted on the district's web site along with other printed materials related to bullying and harassment prevention.

The regulations for formal complaint procedures and the ability to file a written grievance for discrimination or harassment based on one's disability has been required in schools since the establishment of Section 504 of the Rehabilitation Act of 1973 (PL 93-112). This federal law has always required school districts to designate the people responsible for coordinating compliance with Section 504 and Title II, including the reporting and investigation of any complaints of sexual, gender-based, or disability-based harassment. For assistance in drafting current policies for reporting bullying, school leaders can refer to the formal written requirements from the Section 504 coordinator or designee.

 I too have ADD and have been teased because of it but don't worry it will get better. I have some nice friends and they know I have ADD and they don't tease me about it anymore. My advice is to find some friends who seem nice. If they are good friends, they won't tease you and they will stand up for you.

INVESTIGATING AN INCIDENT OF BULLYING OR HARASSMENT

School leaders from state educational agencies, school superintendents, and local principals should follow universal written procedures based on federal regulations and technical assistance from the U.S. Department of Education for responding to reports of bullying. A designated school official should have expertise in both investigating and determining an incident of bullying and/or disability harassment or potentially a denial of a free appropriate public education (FAPE). As recommended by the U.S. Department of Education (2010),

> school districts should have policies which include a procedure for promptly investigating and responding to any report of an incident of bullying, including immediate intervention strategies for protecting the victim from additional bullying or retaliation, and includes notification to parents of the victim, or reported victim, of bullying and the parents of the alleged perpetrator, and, if appropriate, notification to law enforcement officials. (p. 5)

These written policies and procedures detail the specific action steps that school personnel are mandated to follow consistently across all grade levels, regardless of the student's protected class.

Recently, a school district in California implemented a two-tiered policy and reporting system. One policy and set of procedures was adopted for cases involving harassment of students within "protected classes" (e.g., disability, race, religion, gender, sexual orientation) that would be investigated and resolved following the strict federal guidelines and criteria (Burke, 2013). Another set of procedures was created for students not labeled within a "protected" class. These cases would be handled under a different set of rules at the school level, with fewer procedural protections. This type of two-tiered system for students in protected classes versus "nonprotected" students is not recommended in the U.S. Department of Education's "Anti-Bullying Policies: Examples of Provisions in State Laws" (2010). A two-tiered system creates several problems:

- There is potential for students who may have an unidentified disability or for potential Child Find students to fall through the cracks.

- Students with disabilities who have protections from breaches of confidentiality may not receive the required federal protections due to a lack of awareness for the student's protected status. This means that a staff member may not know the student has a disability and not follow the appropriate set of procedures within the two-tiered system.

- This can involve additional paperwork to an already overburdened school system. A two-tiered system would require two sets of forms and documentation.

- This has potential for dividing parents within the same school who may view a tiered system as offering protections for only certain students, thereby eroding a united positive school climate.

The SST and school leaders can adequately address all incidents of bullying and/or harassment of students with disabilities or other protected classes within a comprehensive policy and investigation protocol that meets with federal regulations, state-level policies, and best practice standards, where all students are provided with equal protection. Some states, like New Jersey, have adopted statutory requirements that are inclusive of both bullying and harassment, which alleviates any confusion.

Investigating an incident of bullying or harassment requires a highly trained school administrator who is well-versed in federal and state regulations and the requirements for responding to and investigating a bullying incident. Although it is true that Individuals with Disabilities Education Act (IDEA) regulations stipulate much greater procedural safeguards that are not legally required for students who qualify solely under Section 504, the U.S. Department of Education, Office of Civil Rights (OCR), has repeatedly underscored a school's obligation to address and prevent disability harassment, regardless of if the student qualifies under IDEA or Section 504 (OCR, 2014). Students who qualify under Section 504 have the same rights to an appropriate public education that is free of bullying and harassment as students who receive special education services under IDEA. The OCR (2010) "reminds schools that failure to recognize discriminatory harassment may lead to inadequate or inappropriate responses that may violate a students' civil rights," regardless of which federal statute applies to the student. Therefore, it is important for schools to evaluate their bullying and harassment prevention policies and procedures to ensure they adequately address all cases of disability harassment for students eligible for IDEA services and for students who qualify under Section 504.

INVESTIGATING AND DETERMINING DISABILITY-BASED HARASSMENT

Not all cases of bullying involving a student with a disability is disability-based harassment or a denial of IDEA FAPE or 504 FAPE—just as not all cases of childhood conflict involve bullying. Complex social interactions require professional judgment, high levels of experience, and effective investigation methods. The following are specific scenarios to demonstrate when an incident can be defined as bullying, disability-based harassment, or a denial of FAPE:

Scenario 1: Bullying

A group of female high school students attend the school's dance team, which is a high school accredited class that meets first period. The same group then participates in the school's color guard, which practices after school with the band. The three cocaptains of the dance and color guard team have started hazing several of the freshmen on the team, including a 15-year-old student with a hearing impairment and a learning disability, who we will call Lauren. The cocaptains require all the freshman girls to carry the equipment and wear their underwear inside out, and they call them derogatory names. An assistant coach witnessed the behavior and asked the cocaptains to stop. The coach did not report the bullying to a school official, and it continued for several months. Lauren's parents noticed a significant change in her behavior at home and questioned her regarding school and dance activities. Lauren told her parents about the abuse, and they wrote a formal complaint to the principal. After an immediate and thorough investigation, the school found grounds of bullying based on the school's written policies and suspended the cocaptains from the team. The school offered counseling to all of the girls on the team, including Lauren. In addition, the assistant coach was removed, and staff training was required for all school personnel. The school carefully monitored any further incidents. In addition, Lauren's individualized education program (IEP) team met to discuss any adverse effects to her educational program but determined that no additional aids or services were necessary. Lauren was receiving educational benefit from her current IEP. Therefore, there was no denial of IDEA FAPE services.

Discussion: Although this incident involved a girl with a disability, she was not harassed based on her disability. The school's prompt and thorough investigation did not find evidence to meet the four-prong criteria for a disability-based harassment violation. The school responded immediately to stop the bullying and carefully monitored all future incidents. There would be no foundation for disability-based harassment. In addition, she was not denied IDEA FAPE services and continued to benefit from her IEP.

Scenario 2: Bullying and a Denial of a Free Appropriate Public Education

Again, the cocaptains of the high school color guard and dance team flagrantly hazed all freshman girls on the team, including Lauren, a 15-year-old student with a hearing impairment and learning disability. The girls were required to drink from a separate water fountain on the other side of the school, wear mismatched clothing, and write vulgar words on their hands and were called derogatory names. Again, the assistant coach observed some of the incidents but did not take decisive action to stop the bullying. Lauren started skipping first period and refused to attend color guard practice after school. Her parents received a notification from the school regarding excessive absences from dance class. Lauren told her parents about the hazing, and the parents filed a complaint with the school. The school immediately took action and determined that bullying and hazing had occurred, which was against the school's code of conduct and policies. School administrators suspended the cocaptains of the team and fired the assistant coach. The school did not find evidence to prove disability-based harassment, as the bullying was not based on the Lauren's disability. Lauren's IEP team did find she had been denied IDEA FAPE, as the bullying caused her to skip dance class, and she was deprived access to educational benefits. Her IEP team reviewed the current plan and found they lacked appropriate goals for teaching social skills or communication goals. The IEP team added supports and services to meet her unique needs, including an interpreter for practice after school. In addition, the IEP team wrote accommodations for the dance class and color guard so that Lauren could adequately hear the coach's instructions. The principal also required ongoing monitoring and supervision to prevent retaliation.

Discussion: In this scenario, Lauren was not targeted based on her disability. In addition, school leaders took immediate action to stop the bullying and monitored for future incidents. The behavior exhibited by the cocaptains of the team was punishable based on the school's written policies for bullying. Even though this scenario did not meet the criteria for a hostile environment and disability-based harassment, the school would still have an obligation to address any FAPE-related concerns (OCR, 2014). Lauren's IEP was no longer designed to provide a meaningful educational benefit and required additional goals and accommodations, which were ultimately addressed.

Scenario 3: Disability-Based Harassment and Denial of a Free Appropriate Public Education

Using the same dance class and color guard example in this scenario, the cocaptains targeted Lauren with abusive demands. They used offensive language such as "idiot" and "retard." They made her turn her back during practices so she had difficulty reading lips and following the choreography. Lauren began skipping first period in order to avoid dance class. The assistant coach was indifferent about the obvious bullying and did not report the incidents to school administration. Lauren's parents received a notice from the school regarding excessive absences, and when confronting their daughter with the school letter, she told them about the harassment. The parents called and spoke with the school principal, who suggested that the parents speak directly to the head coach of the dance team for more information. After several weeks of nonaction by any school leader, the parents filed a formal written complaint of harassment. The investigation found grounds for disability-based harassment, as the evidence supported each of the four-prong criteria. In addition, the IEP team determined the student was denied IDEA FAPE services, as she was receiving a failing grade in dance class and refused to participate in color guard due to the peer abuse. After several weeks, the school responded and suspended the cocaptains of the dance team. The school also agreed to overhaul their reporting system and created an anonymous online system for students to report. Training was required for all staff, including coaching staff. The IEP team reviewed additional supports for Lauren, with the inclusion of an interpreter for practices and additional goals for teaching social-communication skills.

Discussion: This incident involved a student with a disability and met the four-prong criteria for disability-based harassment. In addition, the student was denied IDEA FAPE services due to the harassment that interfered with her ability to benefit from her educational program. As a general rule, "When a student who receives IDEA FAPE Services or 504 FAPE services has experienced bullying resulting in disability-based harassment violation, there is a strong likelihood that the student was denied FAPE" (OCR, 2014, p. 7). Table 8.2 provides steps for investigating a bullying incident and determining disability-based harassment.

Table 8.2.   Procedural steps for an investigation of a bullying incident and determination of disability-based harassment

1. Identify all students involved and assign a case number. Identify any student with disabilities.

2. Contact parents.

3. Conduct an investigation for each incident of bullying or suspected disability harassment in a timely manner (e.g., within 10 school days). Interview students and staff involved in the incident, including all bystanders.

4. Determine if disability harassment has occurred.

5. Provide intensive and targeted interventions to both the victim and the bully or group of bullies (e.g., counseling).

6. Identify corrective measures and implement steps to end harassment, prevent future retaliation, and monitor future incidents.

7. Maintain written documentation of the report form as well as all resolutions.

ACTION STEPS FOR INVESTIGATION

Once the school official or designee receives a report or has reason to believe that a bullying incident has occurred, they must promptly conduct an investigation in accordance with federal and state laws as well as the written procedures adopted by the state and local educational agency. The OCR has provided school leaders with the required actions for investigating an incident of bullying or harassment (OCR, 2010, 2014).

1. *Review disability status:* Upon receiving notification of bullying, regardless of what means (e.g., verbally, written, electronic), the school official must determine if the incident involved a student with a protected category such as a student with a disability. School officials must take immediate action when alerted of an incident of bullying that involves a student with a disability. It is important to remember that anyone can file a report regarding harassment, including the student, parent, or any adult who is aware or concerned regarding a threat to a student with a disability. The OCR (2010) makes clear to schools that "once a school knows or reasonably should know, it must take immediate and appropriate action to investigate or otherwise determine what occurred." Therefore, all staff should be trained to promptly report incidents of bullying to school administrators or the designee within one school day in order to take "immediate" action.

Criminal Activity

A school official or designee should immediately determine if criminal activity has occurred. If so, report to the proper authorities or local police. For example, if physical harm or possible sexual abuse is suspected, police should be notified. School officials should ensure that there is not an ongoing threat of physical violence to a student and take steps to protect any student from harm.

---

2. *Notify parents:* Phone calls or written notification to parents of both the victim and student(s) who have been identified as the bully should take place within one school day of a filed report. Any phone calls should be recorded into a phone log or directly written onto the formal reporting document, with dates and times. Establish open lines of communication with parents and share the exact procedures that will be followed, including specific time lines for the investigation. Refer parents to the school's web site or student code of conduct to clarify school policies and procedures. Avoid labeling students as a "bully" or the "victim." Provide parents with an objective description of the events as documented and avoid editorial comments. Parent notification must not breach confidentiality protections provided by the Family Educational Rights and Privacy Act

(FERPA; PL 93-380). FERPA regulations provide privacy protections to all students and are not specific to students with disabilities. FERPA restricts the nonconsensual disclosure of personally identifiable information from a student's educational record (20 U.S.C.; 1232g.). School officials should seek legal guidance to ensure all federal regulations are consistently implemented with the provisions of this law.

3. *Conduct interviews:* Part of the school policy for investigating an incident of bullying includes a template of suggested questions for the school official designee to follow during an interview. Regardless of the current principal's professional experience or lack of experience, each school must have in place a standard set of questions for all incidents of bullying to minimize gaps or discrepancies within the investigation. Interview questions should be probative and objective but also clear and concrete, keeping in mind that students with disabilities may have significant impairments with auditory processing, communication skills, and emotional disorders that can ultimately affect the investigation. The New Jersey Department of Education has disseminated a practical guide for the application of their statewide Anti-Bullying Bill of Rights Act (2011), which includes the "Essentials of Harassment, Intimidation, Bullying Investigations" protocol (Drew, 2013). This guidance document includes investigation strategies for school leaders in New Jersey but could easily be modified and utilized as a model program for any state or local agency. The following are interview guidelines obtained from the "Essentials of Harassment, Intimidation, Bullying Investigations." For more information, visit the New Jersey Department of Education web site:

*http://www.state.nj.us/education/students/safety/behavior/hib/overview
.shtml*

• School interviews are not police interrogations and should be carefully planned with objective questions that are respectful to all students and appropriate to the age and cognitive level of the students involved in the incident. Great care is given to be empathetic and nonjudgmental, with a focus on utilizing the interview as a teachable moment on kindness, empathy, and bullying prevention. Students with disabilities do not always recognize problem behaviors as bullying, may not understand manipulation or exploitive behavior as harmful, or may be reluctant to stand up for themselves and seek help (U.S. Department of Education, 2013). The school official conducting the interview must not engage in arguing with a student or provide negative comments or perceived aggressive actions during an interview. For example, overt nonverbal body language such as standing over a seated student, accusatory voice tones, and angry facial expressions from an authority figure will impair the investigation and may revictimize the students involved. Keeping in mind that bystanders often witness dreadful acts of bullying and harassment, the school official should avoid revictimizing the students involved.

- Interviews are conducted in private with consideration of student safety. It is not recommended to pull a student out of class and into a hallway with other students ("Were you involved in yesterday's fight after school?"), as this type of public inquiry will lead to a quick no, and the interview will be unproductive. Limit distractions by interviewing students in a private office or designated location, such as the counselor's office.

- Avoid asking simple yes or no questions and probe responses by asking the student to expand: "Did you see any problems on the playground yesterday?" (with a student response of no) versus, "Tell me what happened on the playground yesterday." The purpose of the interview is to reconstruct the events that occurred and to determine the facts of who, what, where, when, and how. Younger students or students with disabilities may require more time in answering questions. They may also need more guidance in formulating answers, but school officials should be cautious about leading students into an answer. For example, "Didn't you see Braden push Jessica into the locker this morning before school?" The student may give the answer the adult wants to hear out of fear. The goal and purpose is to conduct an interview to elicit information in order to determine if bullying or harassment has occurred and the extent of future planning to prevent future incidents while supporting all students.

- According to the federal webinar "Bullying, Harassment, and Civil Rights" (U.S. Department of Education, 2013), a school investigation into disability harassment should encompass the "totality of the circumstances." These include the nature (verbal, physical, relational), scope, frequency, duration, location, relationship to the people involved, incidents outside of school, and the severity of the conduct. A thorough investigation should consider each of these factors when determining if a hostile environment has been created by the incident. Administrators or the school official designee may require training, coaching, feedback, and practice sessions in order to effectively conduct an interview while being sensitive to the emotional status of the students involved.

4. *Review supplementary materials:* The interview process is only part of the investigation. Evidence of disability-based harassment can be discovered through other investigative means. School leaders or the official

designee may review campus videotapes, read student records for a history of bullying incidents, examine physical evidence such as damage to property, or examine other facts gathered from the bullying and harassment report form.

5. *Determine a violation of disability-based harassment:* It is at this point that the school official will determine if the reported incident was 1) normal childhood conflict, such as a harmless prank between peers or aggressive acts between equals; 2) bullying as defined by state and local policies; 3) disability-based harassment as defined by federal regulations; and/ or 4) denial of FAPE (Table 1.4). At the conclusion of the investigation, a school official or review board is required to use professional judgment based on the facts of the individual incident and a thorough review of the evidence and supporting documents. School officials must remain impartial and review only the facts to ensure nondiscriminatory treatment (OCR, 2014). Based on the facts, the school official determines if the allegations and evidence of disability harassment are supported by the investigation. School officials must understand what constitutes normal childhood conflict, bullying, or disability harassment, as these are complex social interactions. Disability-based harassment is defined as unwelcome conduct based on a protected class. It is reasonable to determine that a school official designee will conclude that a reported incident of bullying, such as making threats, taunting, and physical actions involving a victim with a disability, can be harassment, which is unwelcome conduct. According to the federal webinar "Bullying, Harassment, and Civil Rights," name calling and belittling a student with a disability can be considered harassment under federal law, and the nature of the conduct itself must be assessed to determine disability harassment (U.S. Department of Education, 2013). Nonphysical acts such as verbal taunting or social isolation can also meet the standards for creating a hostile school environment. The school official designee must determine if the reported incident or actions create a hostile environment: "A hostile environment may exist even if there are no tangible effects on the student where the harassment is serious enough to adversely affect the student's ability to participate in or benefit from the educational program" (OCR DCL, 2000, p. 2).

As stated by the OCR, a hostile environment does not have to demonstrate "tangible" results such as failing grades or dropping out of school. In the case of *T.K. v. NYC Department of Education* (Cyr, 2012), the courts ruled that "it is not necessary to show that bullying prevented all opportunity for an appropriate education, but only that it is likely to affect the opportunity of the student for an appropriate education." The effects of disability-based harassment caused by a hostile environment may change a student's patterns of participation. For example, say a student

Examples of Disability-Based Harassment

- Several students continually remark out loud to other students during class that a student with dyslexia is "retarded" or "deaf and dumb" and doesn't belong in the class; as a result, the harassed student has difficulty doing work in class and her grades decline.
- Students frequently taunt or belittle a student with intellectual disabilities by mocking and intimidating him, so he does not participate in physical education class.
- The boys' tennis team repeatedly harasses a fellow player because he takes frequent snack breaks and must check his blood sugar levels. The student has diabetes and has a 504 plan due to multiple medical issues. The student refuses to check his sugar levels due to the constant teasing. After months of harassing behaviors witnessed by the assistant coach, the student quits the team.
- A teenager with autism spectrum disorder (ASD) carries all her school materials with her each day because she has difficulty opening her locker between classes. Students repeatedly push her in the hallway and knock her books to the floor. There are several incidents where the student is late for class due to repeated actions from other students. The paraprofessionals working with the young girl have witnessed the pushing in the hallway. The student receives detention for accruing multiple tardies and begins to exhibit high levels of anxiety during the school day, which interferes with her schoolwork.

with a disability refuses to ride the school bus due to ongoing, repeated unwelcome actions by other students on the bus; this can meet the requirements for affecting a student's educational program. It should be noted to school officials that students with disabilities who are repeatedly bullied in school may continue to perform academically but demonstrate psychological concerns such as anger issues, depression, and refusal to go to school; this creates a hostile environment and constitutes a denial of FAPE. The U.S. Department of Education has consistently made clear its position to all school employees of their duty to protect students with disabilities from bullying and harassment and the harm of such incidents (Keegan & Monthie, 2014).

I admire your resilience. I am sure there are others who would befriend you for who you are. Furthermore, don't ever think less of yourself. Being different is a false idea because it is biased in everyone's eyes. You have three choices. 1) Ignore it, 2) Let it shape you, and 3) Learn from it. Choose what's best. Sincerely, Concerned friend

6. *Provide corrective measures:* According to the DCL from the OCR (2010), if disability harassment has been investigated and supported by the evidence, a school is obligated to take specific actions that include the following:

- Promptly end the harassment.

- Eliminate the hostile environment.

- Prevent future incidents.

- Prevent retaliation.

School district personnel must consider corrective measures and craft remedies to prevent future incidents of harassment and eliminate a hostile environment regardless of the bullying policies. Put differently, the unique effects of discriminatory harassment may demand a different response than would other types of bullying (OCR, 2010). The following are possible corrective measures for the school official or designee to consider if an investigation reveals discriminatory harassment, followed by information on disciplinary actions.

- Develop, revise, and publicize new school policies.

- Reinforce and widely publicize that the school will not tolerate harassment.

- Implement staff training specifically addressing disability-based harassment.

- Increase school monitors or adult supervision.

- Limit interactions between the bully (harasser) and victim. Contract with student to "cease and desist" any further contact.

- Provide the victim with additional opportunities to obtain benefit from educational program (e.g., retake a test).

- Provide diversity training for all students with curriculum geared toward disability awareness and tolerance.

- Conduct follow-up surveys that target disability harassment.

- Involve parents and community groups in preventing future harassment.

- Discipline the student who has exhibited bullying behaviors (harasser).

DISCIPLINARY ACTIONS

As discussed throughout this book, the discipline measures, sanctions, or punishment administered to those students who exhibit bullying behaviors should be carefully crafted targeted interventions that focus on teaching appropriate social-emotional learning (SEL) skills and conflict resolution, with a focus on keeping students in school. In addition, harsh discipline measures that impose out-of-school suspensions or expulsions for bullying or harassment likely have a negative impact on the entire school and are often not necessary to meet the corrective measures to prevent future incidents of bullying and harassment. Maintain written documentation of all interviews, phone calls, record reviews, or other measures when investigating a bullying incident. In California, school personnel are required to maintain documentation of complaints and their resolution for a minimum of one review cycle (Cal. Educ. Code § 234.1 [2010]). All facets of the investigation should be documented, and information should be kept organized and confidential. As discussed earlier, each incident of bullying is assigned a case number for follow-up with any future events or retaliation. Organized files, whether online or in print, can assist school leaders or designees to efficiently monitor any future incidents of bullying and harassment. School leaders must develop and consistently implement uniform standards for entry, maintenance, and retrieval of data related to bullying and harassment. If there is a change in school leadership or the designee, the school should have written plans in place to maintain accountability across new leadership. School officials may provide evidence to the families, both the victim and bully, of the facts surrounding the investigation that constitute disability harassment, including corrective measures and school responses within Family Educational Rights and Privacy Act (FERPA) regulations.

School personnel who do not take immediate action or ignore bullying and disability harassment must understand they are violating federal civil rights laws and exposing the school district to litigation. Failure to properly consider that student misconduct can result in disability harassment is a serious liability, as schools are required under federal law to eliminate any hostile environment. School districts can find themselves under federal investigation when complaints of bullying and harassment demonstrate a lack of organized inquiry, failure to interview witnesses, poor record keeping, lack of familiarity with the law, inadequate training, piecemeal approaches, ineffective measures to stop the bullying, and failure to adequately address the effects of a hostile environment created by the actions of the bully. Of course, the threat of litigation should not be the sole reason to develop and implement comprehensive multitiered bullying and harassment prevention programs: School personnel are ultimately responsible for protecting students from harm and creating a safe and civil school environment.

Implementation Checklist

Can you . . . ?   **Yes**

Review school reporting form and assess for standardized components   ☐

Identify staff who are designated to receive and respond to bullying   ☐

Create a bullying report form that is accessible to students with disabilities   ☐

Address concerns associated with false reporting   ☐

Explicitly teach reporting procedures to all students and staff   ☐

Ensure appropriate investigative procedures are followed   ☐

List potential corrective measures   ☐

Sustainable Programs for Reducing Bullying and Harassment

Bullying incidence rates and survey data are powerful change agents for long term sustainability and for reducing future rates of bullying and harassment. Faced with this clear evidence, educators can begin to make important data-based decisions to revise school policies and procedures and create safe learning environments for all students. As previously stated, data-driven practices succeed when teachers analyze their own class data. General districtwide trends in school climates or rates of bullying mean little to the second-grade teacher in one elementary school out of eight schools in the entire district. Each school must analyze and disaggregate the data by grade level and other coded information (e.g., gender, protected class, nature of bullying). Direct assessment data from surveys and incident reports are combined with information from focus groups and other school observations to drive improved outcomes for all students and guide the school in selecting appropriate interventions for future programming. Careful examination and analysis of the individual school's data encourages schools to direct their resources to where they can have the greatest impact in reducing the rates of bullying and eliminate a hostile environment for students with disabilities.

DATA ANALYSIS TO DRIVE IMPROVED OUTCOMES

Data analysis entails collecting, organizing, and interpreting multiple sources of data in order to make effective educational decisions. At first glance, data analysis may appear complicated for classroom teachers or members of the school safety team (SST), as they are not trained statisticians. Data analysis conjures up technical language such as *t* tests, ANOVA (analysis of variance), nonparametric measures, and regressions scores. Fortunately, reliable and valid data analysis does not require complex mathematical equations or complicated designs. Here are a few general guidelines for data analysis:

1. Collect and organize multiple forms of data and summarize findings.

2. Display data for interpretation. Create a visual representation of the summarized data, such as a graph, to differentiate strengths of the overall program and areas for improvement.

3. Generate an annual yearly report that is inclusive of the current data as well as plans for implementation and sustainability.

Multiple forms of data collection have been discussed including surveys, focus groups, and bullying and harassment reporting forms. Once data has been collected, school leaders and the SST must begin organizing the data in a meaningful way for parents, students, staff, and the community. Most school districts purchase computer software and data management systems to organize quantitative data for analysis. Schools generate a variety of reports on attendance, disciplinary actions, and test scores to meet state and federal regulations. Data from climate surveys and student surveys on bullying can also be managed with the school's adopted software program. Survey data, like other forms of school data, is entered directly into a software program to analyze trends, measure outcomes, and guide future planning.

I know a lot of people like you who get made fun of because how they look. They usually just laugh and brush it off. I recommend you do the same. To defeat your enemies, you have to act like it doesn't bother you. I would also recommend joining a club or sports. Next time there is a try-out, go and make new friends. Do not let those ignorant bullies get to you. Remember, you already won by being so strong.

Part of data analysis includes graphing data as a visual representation of progress or for the purposes of identifying areas for improvement. School leaders along with members of the SST summarize and display the data in order to interpret the results and determine trends. Again, most school districts have computer systems that generate reports and visual graphs of the data for future planning. If not, there are many online educational companies that provide technical assistance to school personnel for creating graphs and other types of reports. Simple graphing tools, such as Microsoft Excel, assist school personnel in constructing graphs for the purpose of results-driven accountability and decision making.

Visual graphs can represent student driven activities as part of the schoolwide bullying prevention program. Figure 9.1 is a visual representation of student participation in schoolwide activities by grade level (for sixth to eighth grade). Promoting positive results from student and staff participation is incorporated within an annual yearly report to demonstrate progress and the school's commitment to sustainable effective programs.

With the graphing or other visual representation completed, the SST can now begin to interpret the data and draw conclusions and recommendations. For example, school leaders along with the SST may want to analyze the data from the school's bullying reporting system and the data collected from student surveys. The SST might formulate the following questions for analysis:

1.   What is the total rate of bullying incidents based solely on reporting measures (e.g., the number of bullying incidents reported by students)?

2.   What is the percentage of bullying and harassment based on student surveys (e.g., percentage of students surveyed who experienced bullying in school)?

3.   What is the comparison of reporting data (item 1) and survey data (item 2)?

Figure 9.2 is a graph representing the percentage of students who reported an incident of bullying in the past month (which was approximately 9% of the total student population), compared with the percentage of students who stated

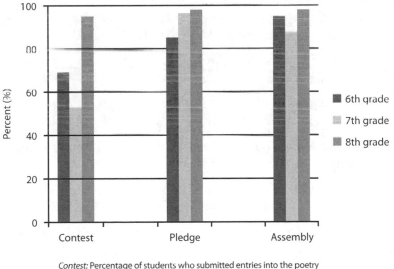

Contest: Percentage of students who submitted entries into the poetry and poster contest for determining the school's anti-bullying motto

Pledge: Percentage of students who participated in the school's pledge drive to the "Spread the Word to End the Word" campaign

Assembly: Percentage of students who participated in the school assembly

Figure 9.1.   Percentage of student participation in schoolwide activities.

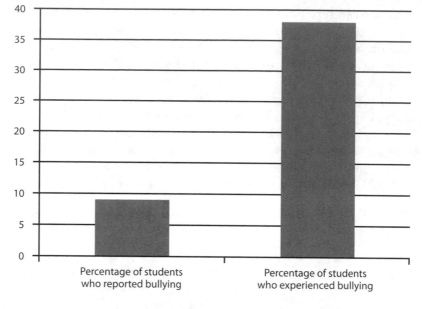

Figure 9.2. Data analysis of comparison data.

they had been bullied in the past month according to student survey data (which was 38% of the student population). The data suggests that students are experiencing higher rates of bullying than is being reported to school personnel. The SST must now delve deeper into the data to determine the reason for this discrepancy and to make recommendations for future interventions. The SST may want to disaggregate the data and analyze the following:

1. What was the rate of bullying broken down into demographics (gender, grade level)?

2. What was the rate of bullying disaggregated for protected classes (race, color, national origin, sex, disability, and religion)?

3. What was the percentage of incidents where adults were present? Did the adults intervene, and what actions were taken?

4. In what percentage of incidents were bystanders present? Did the bystander intervene, and what action was taken?

5. What was the nature or type of bullying (physical, verbal, social exclusion, cyberbullying)?

6. Where did the bullying occur (location of hot spots)?

7. Did students report to an adult? And if not, why?

8. Are there any additional data as highlighted by the individualized survey created by the SST?

It is only through careful examination of all the data that school leaders and the SST can respond to the needs of the students and develop an effective program to address the high rate of bullying as reported from the student survey.

The final step in data analysis is to identify future goals and necessary changes to the current policies and procedures to decrease bullying and harassment in schools. Visual representation or graphing of data will assist the SST, parents, and community stakeholders in identifying patterns and trends from the data. For example, if the analysis or charts suggest that sixth-grade boys are demonstrating higher rates of physical bullying in the cafeteria, then school officials and the SST can plan and implement appropriate interventions to meet the current needs. Interventions include increased supervision in the cafeteria, posting the school anti-bullying rules in a visible location in the cafeteria, and requiring all adults in and around the cafeteria to intervene at the first signs of misbehavior by following the standard operating protocol adopted by the SST. Increasing adult supervision in the cafeteria is a relatively easy and cost-effective remedy to address the findings from the data analysis. Unfortunately, not all revisions and updates to policies and procedures are quite that simple or cost-effective. Intensive professional development for staff or hiring consultants to improve school safety requires additional funding, but the cost-benefit analysis for reducing bullying, improving school climate, and ultimately protecting students from harm is far more important.

There will be a lot of people in life that will try to make you feel small. What you have to do is make yourself feel big! It doesn't matter what others think, as long as you feel powerful, you will be powerful. I wish you well in your journey no matter what path you choose. Sincerely, Your friend

YEARLY REPORT AND TRANSPARENCY

Accountability and transparency are essential components for sustaining programs and building trusting, collaborative relationships with students, parents, and the community. One of the 11 key components recommended by the U.S. Department of Education's "Anti-Bullying Policies: Examples of Provisions in State Laws" (2010) is the requirement for "transparency and monitoring." It is recommended that schools do the following:

- Report annually to the state on the number of reported bullying incidents and any responsive actions taken.

- Make data regarding bullying incidence publicly available in aggregate with appropriate privacy protections to ensure students are protected (Family Educational Rights and Privacy Act [FERPA]; PL 93-380).

This recommended report on bullying and harassment is a careful analysis of the totality of the data, nature or types of bullying, conclusions, and recommendations for future planning. New York State policy (N.Y. Educ. Law § 15, 2010) requires district administration to "provide that such reports shall, wherever possible, also delineate the specific nature of such incidents." Ohio's model policy (§ 3313.666.10, 2010) states that "the district administration . . . [shall] provide . . . a written summary of all reported incidents and post the summary on its web site." Every teacher, school leader, and state educational agency should know the exact number of reported bullying incidents in their state and local school districts as well as corrective measures taken by school leaders. School districts have the technology to generate reports very efficiently; they just need to gather the appropriate data to produce the right reports and make them transparent to parents and the community.

An annual report includes both quantitative and qualitative data in order to generate a document that provides a comprehensive examination of all aspects of bullying and harassment in schools. Reports of qualitative data are composed from responses to open-ended surveys, an executive summary from focus groups, and documentation of student driven activities as well as student-created multimedia materials. The report contains student writing samples (e.g., "Dear Abby" letters), photographs of schoolwide events, video montages of student activities (e.g., poetry contests), and other documents to substantiate the school's ongoing dedication to preventing bullying and harassment. For example, the yearly report may include a calendar of schoolwide events. Table 9.1 identifies student activities that celebrate positive action steps for reducing bullying and harassment.

A combination of quantitative and qualitative data, or mixed methods, helps to substantiate findings and future recommendations. For example, raw quantitative data may not warrant major changes to current school policies and prevention programs (e.g., 6 cases of bullying involving a student with a disability out of 225 students in the school), whereas feedback from parents of children with disabilities from a focus group can provide powerful details and personal accounts of the sometimes severe impact of harassment and the need for changes to the current program. It is important to examine the totality of both

Table 9.1. Annual yearly report: School calendar of anti-bullying activities

Activity	Date
Video of schoolwide assembly for promoting tolerance	September 5
Photographs of all-grade poetry contest	October 9
Letters from community guest speakers on diversity and tolerance in the community	Ongoing monthly
Week of respect activities	November 8
Bully Movie and classroom follow-up activities for bystander education	January 22
Unity day—Photographs of student designed T-shirts	March 3
Peer mentoring luncheon and awards ceremony	April 28

quantitative and qualitative data to have a clear understanding of the issues. The attitudes, opinions, and comments from the students, staff, and parents not only are used to identify gaps and areas for improvement but can also be utilized to identify strengths and to celebrate success.

Although an annual report can be a tool for showing the many positive district-, school-, and classroom-level interventions that have occurred, it may also reveal significant impairments within the overall school safety plan and the gaps in programming to prevent bullying. An annual report may disclose higher rates of bullying or disability-based harassment than predicted. School leaders and teachers are naturally guarded about the high rates of bullying in their schools, which may lead to a lack of transparency, but parents and community stakeholders must demand reporting and transparency of all data related to student safety, including bullying and harassment. A school's annual report that is transparent, widely disseminated, and understandable to students, parents, and stakeholders proves the high level commitment of all school staff to creating a safe school environment where students can learn.

 I understand how difficult it is when kids judge you because It has happened to me. Don't let them discourage you from being yourself. The anger that you have is understandable, and the best way to deal with that would be to talk to a parent or counselor or siblings to cope with all the frustration. Also get rid of the bullies at you school, tell the principal or security at your school. If you ignore them, they will leave you in peace.

SUSTAINABLE BULLYING AND HARASSMENT PREVENTION PROGRAMS

Education, training, awareness campaigns, and community involvement have historically changed cultural norms in a society. We have witnessed major shifts in recycling programs, nonsmoking public facilities, and wearing seat belts that affect everyday practices and routines. Recycling bins, nonsmoking restaurants, and seat belt requirements are now the norm. A permanent cultural change to the social norms or the customary rules that govern behavior in groups requires focused education initiatives, fostering social responsibility, and enforcement of rules (Haines, Perkins, Rice, & Barker, 2005). These same ideals are now being utilized to permanently shift the culture of bullying through multitiered research-based interventions, student-driven activities, social media, and simple acts of kindness. No longer is the silence surrounding bullying deemed a part of normal childhood development. Enduring cultural change requires strict adherence to implementation of the core components of the program, accountability for all staff, and sustainable practices.

Implementation is not a single event; it is a complex, multistep process requiring coordinated planning and staff commitment along with strong school leadership that promotes educational research into routine practices. According to the National Implementation Research Network's *Implementation Research: A Synthesis of the Literature,* implementation is a "set of activities designed to put into practice a program of known dimensions" (Fixsen et al., 2005, p. 5). There are many stages of implementation with defined benchmarks, beginning with an exploration of the current research and ending with long-term sustainable programs. For more detailed information, go to the National Implementation Research Network's web site:

 http://nirn.fpg.unc.edu

 Here is the key to overcoming bullying, you have to overcome your own personal low self-esteem. It is not really about the bullying, although their actions are inexcusable. You don't deserve it, no one does. But the only way you can liberate yourself is to lift your head up high and live your life free of other's opinions.

Successful implementation of an effective bullying and harassment prevention program begins with courageous leadership and administrative support. Superintendents, principals, and other supervisors are a major factor in the initial implementation stages as well as for sustainable outcomes. At the initial stages, school leaders provide the vision along with enthusiasm, resources, and effective professional development to classroom teachers and staff (Fixsen et al., 2005). Effective implementation requires administrators who create a collaborative school team environment that seeks buy-in or a level of commitment from all staff. A lack of staff buy-in is a recognized barrier to long-term implementation and sustainability. According to Cook, Cook, and Landrum (2013), school leaders can increase implementation and teacher buy-in and the level of staff commitment by providing a clear, simple message with tangible measurable outcomes, such as "We are committed to improve school climate and student safety in all areas of the school campus while reducing rates of bullying and harassment by 20 percent in the next 18 months." School leaders must articulate a message that resonates with the school community while deftly moving forward with implementing new programs that are responsive to student needs and overall school safety.

Teachers cannot do anything if you are being bullied. Try to ignore them. If that doesn't work, tell your parents. Also try to walk away from them. The names people call you are terrible. If they punch you, you need to fight back. Don't let anyone put you down. Show compassion for them.

ACCOUNTABILITY STANDARDS

All staff must be held accountable for consistently implementing and adhering to state laws, district policies, and school procedures with regard to bullying and harassment prevention and interventions. As with any large-scale cultural change, there are often federal, state, and local requirements to comply with new laws or policies. For example, wearing one's seat belt saves lives, is a positive step for driver safety, and is the law. Most states require seat belts and have adopted "Click It or Ticket" laws that are not optional for the driver. In much the same way, school leaders must hold all staff accountable for implementing new policies, procedures, and interventions that are not optional. Nowhere is accountability more important than when it comes to protecting vulnerable populations such as students with disabilities who may not be able to protect themselves. Failure to implement and follow federal, state, and local regulations and policies can leave lasting harmful effects. School leaders must identify and hold accountable those individual staff members who are not implementing or adhering to the adopted policies and standard protocols. Follow-up interventions with individual staff members may include additional professional development, intensive coaching, and explicit feedback to ensure accountability and implementation.

Accountability is improved when school leaders along with members of the SST create an auditing checklist to assess implementation fidelity. Auditing checklists have been part of the fabric of school safety planning for decades. School leaders, along with experts in the field of school security, have formulated strict standards for ensuring adherence to school safety plans. Auditing checklists are commonly used in schools to address a variety of safety issues (e.g., evacuation and lockdown procedures), and the same rigid accountability standards should be applied to preventing and responding to bullying and harassment. An auditing checklist emphasizes the universal implementation of state regulations or an adopted prevention program. The New Jersey Department of Education has created and disseminated an auditing checklist to ensure every school is in compliance with state regulations. The New Jersey Harassment, Intimidation, and Bullying Compliance Checklist may be utilized by school leaders as a template for creating a document to meet the unique needs of their school. This extensive checklist (see Appendix F for a sample checklist) contains policy requirements, professional development standards, and reporting procedures. To review the entire compliance checklist, go to the New Jersey Department of Education web site:

http://www.state.nj.us/education/students/safety/behavior/hib/checklist.pdf

This auditing checklist is used to conduct random audits, either electronically or in print, throughout the school year with all or a sampling of staff. The results of the audits are then incorporated into the annual report for transparency with stakeholders.

Auditing checklists are not the only tool utilized for ensuring implementation fidelity; parental engagement is an essential component. Without parental involvement and demands for accountability, school districts may lack sufficient evidence to demonstrate a high degree of student safety standards. One way parents are demanding school accountability for preventing bullying and harassment is through litigation. "Bullying lawsuits are on the rise nationwide," according to General Counsel Francisco Negron, National School Boards Association (DiBlassio, 2011). Parents are using litigation to change the culture of schools through increasing legal action in cases of bullying and harassment. When faced with a lawsuit due to bullying and harassment that leads to serious student safety concerns, even suicide, school leaders and teachers cannot hide behind a policy that does not include strict implementation, transparency, and accountability of evidence-based interventions. Litigation is not the solution to reform school policies and procedures, but parents may feel powerless to change a system that is often in denial of the facts and negative impact of bullying in schools.

 Being different is great! Individuality makes a person feel unique. Love yourself because you are the best in the world. Try talking to school staff about getting bullies away from you because the last thing you want is to get in trouble y the school. Don't ever forget you have value and worth so much.

SUSTAINABILITY STANDARDS

Sustainability is the endurance of a system over long periods of time and the final stage of implementation. New educational programs can often start out with a bang but end in a whimper. Many schools are faced with the presence of competing educational initiatives that make sustainability a challenging proposition. There are measures that can enhance sustainability in schools. First, data-based decision making and results-driven accountability are important for ongoing sustainability. There is a strong correlation among data-based decision making, continuous improvement, and sustainability (McIntosh et al., 2013). Data collection and analysis assists school personnel in focusing on measurable outcomes and the consequences of their policies and procedures. School leaders and teachers are often focused on high-stakes testing and do not recognize the importance of cultivating a positive school climate and decreasing the prevalence of bullying. Shifting a societal norm and complex social issue like the *culture of silence* takes considerable time and commitment to establish positive sustained results. Sustainability is the final and most important step for a permanent cultural shift in the prevention of bullying and harassment.

The second factor in facilitating sustainability is a strong team of school professionals, parents, and students working collaboratively toward a common mission with measurable outcomes. School district administrators clearly communicate the vision and objectives for the program as well as provide resources for every stage of implementation. Teachers must make an investment with a high degree of commitment to stop bullying in schools. The SST is an integral part of implementation and sustainability, but its membership may change: Staff members on the SST may transfer schools or the parent representative may move up to high school when his or her child does, but the long-term survival of an effective multitiered program is based on sustained routine practices (e.g., monthly SST meetings with an agenda and action steps), traditions (e.g., bystander education programs), and required accountability standards (e.g., auditing checklists). It is important to remember that without student engagement, sustained and effective intervention practices are not possible.

Finally, failure to implement and sustain an effective bullying prevention program is not an option. Student dropout rates, low academic achievement, and the long-term mental health effects of bullying affect the entire community. A school is only a microcosm for the larger issues within a society. If the rates of bullying in schools continue to increase in prevalence and school incidence rates are not decreasing, the onus is on the larger community to address the issues and attitudes for tolerance and diversity. Just as the 3 Rs of *Reading, 'Riting, and 'Rithmetic* have been the core components that have sustained our educational system for the last four centuries, the 3 Rs for preventing bullying and harassment will carry us into the future: *Recognize, Respond, and Report.*

 I understand what you are going through but remember you are not alone and everything will be okay. Be proud of who you are, it makes you YOU. Stay truthful to who you are and stay positive. You have a friend in me, and I know what you are going through.

Implementation Checklist

Can you . . . ?	Yes
Describe a mixed methods approach for data collection and highlight the need for qualitative data (e.g., focus group summaries)	☐
Prepare a visual representation or graph of bullying data	☐
Design a school portfolio to capture the multitiered bullying prevention activities	☐
Communicate to stakeholders the need for transparency and annual reporting	☐
Develop an auditing checklist for accountability	☐
Ensure the sustainability of the SST and schoolwide interventions	☐

References

Ability Path. (2011). *Walk a mile in their shoes: Bullying and the child with special needs*. Retrieved from http://www.abilitypath.org/areas-of-development/learning--schools/bullying/articles/walk-a-mile-in-their-shoes.pdf

Agatson, P. (2014). *Suggested guidelines for selecting anti bullying assemblies*. Retrieved from http://cyberbullyhelp.com/recommended-guidelines-for-bullying-prevention-assemblies-patti-agatston-phd/

Alsaker, F., & Valkanover, S. (2012). The Bernese program against victimization in kindergarten and elementary school. In D. Strohmeier & G. Noam (Eds.), *Evidence-based bullying prevention programs for children and youth* (pp. 15–28). San Francisco, CA: Jossey-Bass.

American Educational Research Association. (2013) *Prevention of bullying in schools, colleges, and universities: Research report and recommendations*. Washington, DC: American Educational Research Association.

Americans with Disabilities Amendments Act (ADA) of 2008, PL 110-325, S 3406.

Bambrick-Santoyo, P. (2010). *Driven by data: A practical guide to improve instruction*. San Francisco, CA: Jossey-Bass.

Beane, A. (2009). *Bullying prevention for schools*. San Francisco, CA: Jossey-Bass.

Beebe, J. (2014). Sticks and stones: Using curriculum to stop bullying. *Science Daily*. Retrieved from http://www.sciencedaily.com/releases/2014/01/140127141549.htm

Bogart, L., Elliot, M., Klein, D., Tortolero, S., Mrug, S., Peskin, M., . . . Schuster, E. (2014). Peer victimization in fifth grade and health in tenth grade. *Pediatrics*. doi:10.1542/peds.2013-3510

Borba, M. (n.d.). Bully-proofing our kids. Retrieved from http://www.micheleborba.com/Pages/ArtBMI03.htm

Brackett, M., & Rivers, S. (2014). Preventing bullying with emotional intelligence. *Education Week*. Retrieved from http://www.edweek.org/ew/articles/2014/02/19/21brackett_ep.h33.html?qs=School+Climate,+Health+and+Student+Life

Bradley, R. (2014). Multitiered behavioral support frameworks and social and emotional learning. Federal Bullying Summit 2014. Retrieved from http://www.c-span.org/video/?321013-3/bullying-prevention-summit-social-emotional-learning

Bradshaw, C., Sawyer, A., & O'Brennan, L. (2007). Bullying and peer victimization at school: Perceptual differences between students and school staff. *School Psychology Review, 36*(3), 361–382.

Bradshaw, C., Waasdorp, T., O'Brennan, L., & Gulemietova, M. (2013). Teachers and education support professionals' perspectives on bullying and prevention: Findings from a National Education Association study. *School Psychology Review, 42*(3), 280–297.

Bronfenbrenner, U. (1977). Toward an experimental ecology of human development. *American Psychologist, 32*, 513–531.

Buhs, E., & de Guzman, M. (2007). *Bullying and victimization: What adults can do to help.* Lincoln, NE: University of Nebraska–Lincoln. Retrieved from http://www.extension.unl.edu/c/document _library/get_file?folderId=221677&name=DLFE-3202.pdf

Burke, E. (2013). Palo Alto's new two-tiered bullying policy: Will kids fall through the cracks? Retrieved from http://www.paloaltoonline.com/blogs/p/2013/11/18/palo-altos-new-two-tiered -bullying-policy-will-kids-fall-through-the-cracks-part-1-of-2

California Department of Education. (n.d.). *California healthy kids survey: Student well-being in California.* San Francisco, CA: WestEd Health and Human Development Program.

Carroll, C., Patterson, M., Wood, S., Booth, A., Rick, J., & Balin, S. (2007). A conceptual framework for implementation fidelity. *Implementation Science, 2,* 40. Retrieved from http://www.ncbi.nlm .nih.gov/pmc/articles/PMC2213686

Carter, E., Asmus, J., Moss, C., Cooney, M., Weir, K., Vincent, L., . . . Fesperman, E. (2013). Peer network strategies to foster social connections among adolescents with and without severe disabilities. *Teaching Exceptional Children,* November/December, 51–58.

Center for Parent Information and Resources. (2003). You are your child's first lifelong advocate. Retrieved from http://www.parentcenterhub.org/repository/first-advocate

Charach, A., Pepler, D., & Ziegler, S. (1995). Bullying at school: A Canadian perspective. *Education Canada, 35,* 12–18.

Cohen, J. (2006). Social, emotional, ethical, and academic education: Creating a climate for learning, participation in democracy, and well-being. *Harvard Educational Review, 76*(2), 201–213.

Cohen, J. (2014). School climate policy and practice trends: A paradox. A commentary. *Teachers College Record,* February 21, 2014. Retrieved from http://www.schoolclimate.org/publications/ documents/SCPolicy&PracticeTrends-CommentaryTCRecord2-28-14.pdf

Cohen, J. (n.d.). School climate improvement and breaking the bully-victim-bystander cycle. Retrieved from http://www.schoolclimate.org/prevention/documents/bully-prevention-research -what-works.pdf

Cohen, J., & Freiberg, A. (2013). School climate and bullying prevention. In T. Dary & T. Pickeral (Eds.), *School climate practices for implementation and sustainability.* A school climate practice brief, number 1 (47–51). New York, NY: National School Climate Center.

Cole, S., Eisner, A., Gregory, M., & Ristuccia, J. (2013). *Creating and advocating for trauma-sensitive schools.* Boston, MA: Massachusetts Advocates for Children.

Cole, S., O'Brien, J., Gadd, M., Ristuccia, J., Wallace, D., & Gregory, M. (2005). *Helping traumatized children learn: Supportive school environments for children traumatized by family violence.* Boston, MA: Massachusetts Advocates for Children.

Collett-Klingenberg, L., & Franzone, E. (2008). *Overview of social narratives.* Madison, WI: National Professional Development Center on Autism Spectrum Disorders, Waisman Center, University of Wisconsin.

Coloroso, B. (2008). *The bully, the bullied, and the bystander.* New York, NY: Harper Collins.

Committee for Children. (2001/2005). *Steps to respect: A bullying prevention program.* Seattle, WA: Committee for Children.

Committee for Children. (2008). *Second step: Student success through prevention program.* Seattle, WA: Committee for Children.

Cook, B., Cook, L., & Landrum, T. (2013). Moving research into practice: Can we make dissemination stick? *Exceptional Children, 79*(2), 163–180.

Craig, S. (2008). *Reaching and teaching children who hurt.* Baltimore, MD: Paul H. Brookes Publishing Co.

Cross, R. (2013). Integrating SEL in curriculum and instruction: Aligning SEL with common core state standards and the Danielson framework. Retrieved from http://safesupportivelearning.ed .gov/sites/default/files/SEL%20Webinar.pdf

Cyr, T. (2011). Disability based bullying: Using *T.K. v. NYC Department of Education* as a tool to understand a school's liability. Retrieved from http://www.edlawsoup.com/journal/2012/1/5/ disability-based-bullying-using-tk-v-nyc-dept-of-education-a.html

Davis, S., & Nixon, C. (2014). *Youth voice project: Student insights into bullying and peer mistreatment.* Champaign, IL: Research Press.

DiBlassio, N. (2011). More bullying cases have parents turning to courts. Retrieved from http:// usatoday30.usatoday.com/news/education/story/2011-09-11/bullying-lawsuits-parents-self-defense -courts/50363256/1

Dreiblatt, M. (2008). Strategies to stop bullying, cyberbullying, and social aggression. Retrieved from http://standuptobullying.net/blog/bullying-articles

Drew, A. (2013). Essentials of harassment, intimidation, bullying investigations. Retrieved from http://www.state.nj.us/education/students/safety/behavior/hib/TheInvestigation.pdf

Dryfoos, J.G. (2000). *Evaluations of community schools: Findings to date.* Washington, DC: Coalition for Community Schools. Retrieved from http://www.communityschools.org/assets/1/AssetManager/Evaluation%20of%20Community%20Schools_joy_dryfoos.pdf

Duncan, A. (2010). The myths about bullying: Secretary Arne Duncan remarks at the bullying prevention summit. Retrieved from http://www.ed.gov/news/speeches/myths-about-bullying-secretary-arne-duncans-remarks-bullying-prevention-summit

Durlak, J.A., Weissberg, R.P., Dymnicki, A.B., Taylor, R.D., & Schellinger, K.B. (2011). The impact of enhancing students' social and emotional learning: A meta-analysis of school-based universal interventions. *Child Development, 82,* 405–432.

Eaton, D., Kann, L., Kinchen, S., Shanklin, S., Flint, K., Hawkins, J., . . . Wechsler, H. (2011). Youth risk behavior surveillance. Retrieved from http://www.ncbi.nlm.nih.gov/pubmed/22673000

Epstein, J.L. (2009). *School, family, and community partnerships: Your handbook for action, 3rd edition.* Thousand Oaks, CA: Corwin Press.

Espelage, D.L. (2014). Ecological theory: Preventing youth bullying, aggression, and victimization. *Theory into Practice, 53,* 257–264.

Espelage, D. L. (2014). Psychologist offers insight on bullying and how to prevent it. American Psychological Association. Retrieved from http://newswise.com/articles/view/623873

Espelage, D.L., Polanin, J., & Low, S. (2014). Teacher and staff perceptions of school environment as predictors of student aggression, victimization, and willingness to intervene in bullying situations. *School Psychology Quarterly, 29*(3), 387–405.

Espelage, D.L., Rose, C.A., & Polanin, J.R. (2015). Social-emotional learning program to reduce bullying, fighting, and victimization among middle school students with disabilities. *Remedial and Special Education.* doi:10.1177/0741932514564564

Family Educational Rights and Privacy Act (FERPA) of 1974, PL 93-380, 20 U.S.C., §§ 1232g et seq.

Farrington, D., & Ttofi, M. (2010). School-based programs to reduce bullying and victimization. *Campbell Systematic Reviews, 6.* doi:10.4073/csr.2009.6

Federal Partner in Bullying Prevention Series. (2013). Moving from awareness to action in bullying prevention: Training resources for the field. Retrieved from http://www.stopbullying.gov/blog/2013/08/19/2012-2013-webinar-series-review

Fink, K. (2014). The Common Core standards can succeed if supported by a school climate engaging the whole child. *School Climate Matters, 8*(1), 4–5.

Fixsen, D., Naoom, S., Blasé, K., Friedman, R., & Wallace, F. (2005). *Implementation research: A synthesis of the literature.* Tampa, FL: University of South Florida, National Implementation Research Network (FMHI publication 231).

Franzone, E. (2009). *Overview of naturalistic interventions.* Madison, WI: National Professional Development Center on Autism Spectrum Disorders, Waisman Center, University of Wisconsin.

Franzone, E., & Collet-Klingenberg, L. (2008). *Overview of video modeling.* Madison, WI: National Professional Development Center on Autism Spectrum Disorders, Waisman Center, University of Wisconsin.

Gage, N., Prykanowski, D., & Larson, A. (2014). School climate and bullying victimization: A latent growth model analysis. *School Psychology Quarterly, 29*(3), 256–271.

Ganz, J.B. (2007). Using visual script interventions to address communication skills. *Teaching Exceptional Children, 40*(2), 54–58.

Gavigan, K., & Kurtts, S. (2011). Using children's and young adult literature in teaching acceptance and understanding of individual differences. *The Delta Gamma Bulletin, 77*(2), 11–16.

Gladden, R.M., Vivolo-Kantor, A.M., Hamburger, M.E., & Lumpkin, C.D. (2014). *Bullying surveillance among youths: Uniform definitions for public health and recommended data elements.* Atlanta, GA: Centers for Disease Control and Prevention, National Center for Injury Prevention and Control, and U.S. Department of Education.

Graham, S. (2011). Bullying: A module for teachers. American Psychological Association. Retrieved from http://www.apa.org/education/k12/bullying.aspx

Gray, C. (1995). Teaching children with autism to "read" social situations. In K. Quill (Ed.), *Teaching children with autism: Strategies to enhance communication and socialization* (pp. 219–241). Albany, NY: Delmar.

Gregory, A., Bell, J., & Pollock, M. (2014). How educators can eradicate disparities in school discipline. Discipline Disparities Series. Retrieved from http://www.indiana.edu/~atlantic/wp-content/uploads/2014/03/Disparity_Interventions_Full_031214.pdf

Haines, M., Perkins, H., Rice, R., & Barker, G. (2005). A guide to marketing social norms for health promotion in school and communities. National Social Norms Resource Center. Retrieved from http://www.socialnormsresources.org/pdf/Guidebook.pdf

Hamburger, M.E., Basile, K.C., & Vivolo, A.M. (2011). *Measuring bullying victimization, perpetration, and bystander experiences: A compendium of assessment tools.* Atlanta, GA: Centers for Disease Control and Prevention, National Center for Injury Prevention and Control.

Hefling, K. (2014). Despite increased security, school shootings continue. Retrieved from http://www.pbs.org/newshour/rundown/despite-increased-security-school-shootings-continue/

Hertz, M., Donato, I., & Wright, J. (2013). Bullying and suicide: A public health approach. *Journal of Adolescent Health, 53,* 51–53.

Hinduja, S., & Patchin, J. (2015). *Bullying beyond the schoolyard: Preventing and responding to cyberbullying.* Thousand Oaks, CA: Corwin.

Hong, J.S., & Espelage, D.L. (2012). A review of research on bullying and peer victimization in school: An ecological systems analysis. *Aggression and Violent Behavior, 17,* 311–312. doi:10.1016/j.avb.2012.03.003

Idsoe, T., Dyregrov, A., & Cosmovici-Idsoe, E. (2012). Bullying and PTSD symptoms. *Journal of Abnormal Psychology, 40,* 901–911.

Illinois State Board of Education. (2006). Illinois learning standards: Social/emotional learning. Retrieved from http://www.isbe.net/ils/social_emotional/standards.htm

Individuals with Disabilities Education Improvement Act (IDEA) of 2004, PL 108-446, 20 U.S.C. §§ 1400 *et seq.*

Interactive Autism Network. (2012). IAN research report: Bullying and children with ASD. Retrieved from http://www.iancommunity.org/cs/ian_research_reports/ian_research_report_bullying

Janney, R., & Snell, M. (2006). *Social relationships and peer support* (2nd ed.). Baltimore, MD: Paul H. Brookes Publishing Co.

Juvonen, J., Wang, Y., & Espinoza, G. (2011). Bullying experiences and compromised academic performance across middle school grades. *Journal of Early Adolescence.* doi:10.1177/0272431610379415

Juvonen, J., Wang, Y., & Espinoza, G. (2013). Physical aggression, spreading rumors, and social prominence in early adolescence: Reciprocal effects supporting gender similarities. *Journal of Youth and Adolescence, 42,* 1801–1810.

Keegan, J., & Monthie, J. (2014). Bullying and harassment of students with disabilities. Retrieved from http://bianys.org/_literature_132500/Webinar_Bullying_Slides

Kowalski, R., Limber, S., & Agatston, P. (2012). *Cyberbullying: Bullying in the digital age.* West Sussex, UK: Wiley-Blackwell.

Kraemer, J. (2010). School bus bullying: The road to safer, calmer school bus environments. Retrieved from http://public-groups.nea.org/legacy/file_cabinet/download/0x00004548f

Langevin, M., Bortnick, K., Hammer, T., & Wiebe, E. (1998). Teasing/bullying experienced by children who stutter: Toward development of a questionnaire. *Contemporary Issues in Communication Science and Disorders, 25,* 12–24.

Latane, B., & Darley, J. (1968). Group inhibition of bystander intervention in emergencies. *Journal of Personality and Social Psychology, 10*(3), 215–221.

Limber, S., & Snyder, M. (2006). What works and doesn't work in bullying prevention and intervention. *The State Education Standard,* July. Retrieved from http://www.yaleruddcenter.org/resources/upload/docs/what/bias/educators/Educators-NASBEBullyingArticle.pdf

Magg, J., & Katsiyannis, A. (2012). Bullying and students with disabilities: Legal and practice considerations. *Behavioral Disorders, 37*(2), 78–86.

Markowitz, N. (2013). The collaborative for reaching and teaching the whole child. Retrieved from http://reachandteachthewholechild.org/189-2/

Marr, N., & Field, T. (2001). *Bullycide: Death at playtime.* Oxfordshire, UK: Success Unlimited.

Massachusetts Department of Elementary and Secondary Education. (2011). Addressing the needs of students with disabilities in the IEP and in school bullying prevention and intervention efforts. Retrieved from http://www.doe.mass.edu/bullying/considerations-bully.html

McEvoy, A. (2005). *Teachers who bully students: Patterns and policy implications.* Presented at the Hamilton Fish Institutes Persistently Safe Schools Conference, Philadelphia, September 11, 2005.

McIntosh, K., Mercer, S.H., Hume, A.E., Frank, J.L., Turri, M.G., & Mathews, S. (2013). Factors associated with sustained implementation of schoolwide positive behavior support. *Exceptional Children, 79,* 293–311.

Merrell, K. (2007). *Strong kids: A social and emotional learning curriculum.* Baltimore, MD: Paul H. Brookes Publishing Co.

Moalem, S. (2014). *Inheritance: How our genes change our lives—and our lives change our genes.* New York, NY: Grand Central Publishing.

Monahan, M. (2013). Teacher aggression: An attempt to dialogue. In M. O'Moore & P. Stevens (Eds.), *Bullying in Irish education* (pp. 227–261). Cork, Ireland: Cork University Press.

Nansel, T., Overpeck, M., Pilla, R., Ruan, W., Simons-Morton, B., & Scheidt, P. (2001). Bullying behaviors among US youth: Prevalence and association with psychological adjustment. *Journal of the American Medical Association, 285*(16), 2094–2100.

National Association of School Psychologists. (2010). Zero tolerance and alternative strategies: A fact sheet for educators and policymakers. Retrieved from http://www.nasponline.org/resources/factsheets/zt_fs.aspx

National Association of School Psychologists. (2012). *A framework for schoolwide bullying prevention and safety.* Bethesda, MD: National Association of School Psychologists. Retrieved from http://www.nasponline.org/resources/bullying/bullying_brief_12.pdf

National Autism Center. (2009). Evidence based practice and autism in the schools. Retrieved from http://www.nationalautismcenter.org/resources/for-educators/

National Center for Education Statistics. (2008). Indicators of school crime and safety. Retrieved from http://nces.ed.gov/pubsearch/pubsinfo.asp?pubid=2009022

National Center for Education Statistics. (2011). Indicators of School Crime and Safety: 2011. Retrieved from http://nces.ed.gov/pubs2012/2012002rev.pdf

National Center for Education Statistics. (2013). Indicators of school crime and safety: 2012. Retrieved from https://nces.ed.gov/pubsearch/pubsinfo.asp?pubid=2014042

National Crime Victimization Survey. (2011). Student reports of bullying and cyber-bullying: Results from the 2011 school crime supplement to the national crime victimization survey. Retrieved from http://nces.ed.gov/pubs2013/2013329.pdf

National Education Association. (2010). How to identify bullying. Retrieved from https://www.nea.org/home/53359.htm

National Education Association. (n.d.). The NEA bullying prevention kit: What is bullying? Retrieved from http://www.nea.org/home/neabullyfree.html

National Parent Teacher Association. (n.d.). Resolution against bullying. Retrieved from http://www.pta.org/programs/content.cfm?ItemNumber=943

National School Climate Council. (2007). The school climate challenge: Narrowing the gap between school climate research and school climate policy, practice guidelines and teacher education policy. Retrieved from http://www.schoolclimate.org/climate/documents/policy/school-climate-challenge-web.pdf

Neitzel, J., & Busick, M. (2009). *Overview of self-management.* Chapel Hill, NC: National Professional Development Center on Autism Spectrum Disorders, Frank Porter Graham Child Development Institute, University of North Carolina.

Network of Autism Training and Technical Assistance Program. (2013). Bullying and students on the autism spectrum. Retrieved from http://www.iidc.indiana.edu/?pageId=3587

New Jersey Department of Education. (2011). Anti-bullying bill of rights act: Essentials of harassment, intimidation, bullying investigations. Retrieved from http://www.state.nj.us/education/students/safety/behavior/hib/

Nikopoulos, C.K., & Keenan, M. (2007). Using video modeling to teach children with autism. *Journal of Autism and Developmental Disorders, 37,* 678–693.

Noddings, N. (2014). Social emotional learning through kindness in the classroom. The Random Acts of Kindness Foundation. Retrieved from http://www.randomactsofkindness.org/kindness-in-the-classroom

O'Connell, P., Pepler, D., & Craig, W. (1999). Peer involvement in bullying: Insights and challenges for intervention. *Journal of Adolescence, 22,* 437–452.

Olweus, D. (1993). *Bullying at schools.* Malden, MA: Blackwell Publishing.

Pepler, D., & Craig, W. (2000). Making a difference in bullying. Retrieved from http://peacefulschoolsinternational.org/wp-content/uploads/making_a_difference_in_bullying.pdf

Polanin, J., Espealage, D., & Pigott, T. (2012). A meta-analysis of school-based bullying prevention programs' effects on bystander intervention behavior. *School Psychology Review, 41*(1), 47–65.

Ragozzino, K., & Utne-O'brien, M. (2009). Social and emotional learning and bullying prevention. Retrieved from http://www.casel.org/s/3_SEL_and_Bullying_Prevention_2009.pdf

Rath, T., & Clifton, D. (2004). *How full is your bucket?* New York, NY: Gallup Press.

Rehabilitation Act of 1973, PL 93-112, 29 U.S.C. §§ 701 *et seq.*

Reiney, E., & Harrington, K. (2012). Moving from awareness to action in bullying prevention. Federal Partners Webinar Series. Retrieved from http://www.stopbullying.gov/what-is-bullying/webinar.html

Reiney, E., & Limber, S. (2013). Why we don't use the word "bully" to label kids. Retrieved from http://www.stopbullying.gov/blog/2013/10/23/why-we-don%25E2%2580%2599t-use-word>-%25E2%2580%259Cbully%25E2%2580%259D-label-kids

Richardson, A. (2014). Bullying incidents low in Upper Township schools. *Shore News Today.* Retrieved from http://www.shorenewstoday.com/snt/news/index.php/upper-township/upper-township/58492-bullying-incidents-low-in-upper-township-schools-report-says.html

Rimm-Kaufman, S., Larsen, R., Baroody, A., Curby, T., Ko, M., Thomas, J., . . . DeCoster, J. (2014). Efficacy of the responsive classroom approach: Results from a 3-year, longitudinal randomized controlled trial. *American Educational Research Journal.* doi:10.3102/0002831214523821. Retrieved from http://aer.sagepub.com/content/early/2014/02/21/0002831214523821.full

Rivers, I., Poteat, V., Noret, N., & Ashurst, N. (2009). Observing bullying at school: The mental health implications of witness status. *School Psychology Quarterly, 24*(4), 211–223.

Robers, S., Zhang, J., Truman, J., & Snyder, T.D. (2012). *Indicators of school crime and safety: 2011* (pub no. NCES 2012–002/NCJ 236021). Washington, DC: U.S. Department of Education and U.S. Department of Justice. Retrieved from http://nces.ed.gov/pubs2012/2012002.pdf

Rooke, J. (n.d.). The father of anti-bullying programs: Born in Sweden. Retrieved from http://www.latitudenews.com/story/the-father-of-anti-bullying-programs-born-in-sweden/

Rose, C. (2013). The bully and the bullied: Tiered intervention and supports. Council for Exceptional Children. Retrieved from http://www.cec.sped.org/Professional-Development/Events-Calendar/2013/10/WEBSRS1305

Rose, C., & Espelage, D. (2012). Risk and protective factors associated with bullying the involvement of students with emotional and behavioral disorders. *Behavioral Disorders, 37,* 133–148.

Rose, C., & Monda-Amaya, L. (2011). Bullying and victimization among students with disabilities: Effective strategies for classroom teachers. *Intervention in School and Clinic.* doi:10.1177/1053451211430119

Rose, C.A., Monda-Amaya, L.E., & Espelage, D.L. (2011). Bullying perpetration and victimization in special education: A review of the literature. *Remedial and Special Education, 32,* 114–130. doi:10.1177/0741932510361247

Rose, C., Swearer, S., & Espelage, D. (2012). Bullying and students with disabilities: The untold narrative. *Focus on Exceptional Children, 45*(2), 1–10.

Ross, S., Horner, R., & Stiller, B. (2008). Bullying prevention in positive behavior supports. Retrieved from http://www.pbis.org/common/cms/files/pbisresources/bullyprevention_es.pdf

Rossen, E., & Cowan, K.C. (2012). *A framework for school-wide bullying prevention and safety.* Bethesda, MD: National Association of School Psychologists.

Salmivalli, C. (2010). Bullying and the peer group: A review. *Aggression and Violent Behavior, 15,* 112–120.

Sentenac, M., Gavin, A., Arnaud, C., Molcho, M., Godeau, E., & Gabhainn, S. (2011). Victims of bullying among students with a disability or chronic illness and their peers. *Journal of Adolescent Health, 48,* 461–466. doi: http://dx.doi.org/10.1016/j.jadohealth.2010.07.031

Sigafoos, J., O'Reilly, M., & de la Cruz, B. (2007). *How to use video modeling and video prompting.* Austin, TX: Pro-Ed.

Skiba, R. (2013). School discipline at a crossroads: Issues of effectiveness and equity. Supportive School Discipline Webinar Series. Retrieved from http://safesupportivelearning.ed.gov/events/webinar/making-case-positive-approaches-discipline

Skiba, R., Reynolds, C., Graham, S., Sheras, P., Conoley, J., & Garcia-Vazquez, E. (2006). Are zero tolerance policies effective in the schools? An evidentiary review and recommendations. American Psychological Association. doi:10.1037/0003-066X.63.9.852. Retrieved from http://www.apa.org/pubs/info/reports/zero-tolerance.pdf

Snyder, T. (2014). A look at bullying data: Indicators of school crime and safety. Federal Bullying Prevention Summit 2014. Retrieved from http://www.c-span.org/video/?321013-6/bullying-prevention-summit-part-2

Srabstein, J. (2014). State and federal laws, policies, and guidance. Federal Bullying Prevention Summit 2014. Retrieved from http://www.c-span.org/video/?321013-6/bullying-prevention-summit-part-2

Starkey, P., & Klein, A. (2000). Fostering parental support for children's mathematical development: An intervention with head start families. *Early Education and Development, 11*(5), 659–680.

Steffgen, G., Recchia, S., & Viechtbauer, W. (2013). The link between school climate and violence in school: A meta-analytic review. *Aggression and Violent Behavior, 18*(2).

Sterzing, P., Shattuck, P., Narendorf, S., Wagner, M., & Cooper, B. (2012). Prevalence and correlates of bullying involvement among adolescents with an autism spectrum disorder. *Archives of Pediatrics & Adolescent Medicine, 166*(11), 1058–1064. doi:10.1001/archpediatrics.2012.790

Stiller, B., Nese, R., Tomlanovich, A., Horner, R., & Ross, S. (2013). Bullying and harassment prevention in positive behavior support: Expect respect. Retrieved from http://www.pbis.org/common/cms/files/pbisresources/2013_02_18_final_covr_manual_123x.pdf

Strohmeier, D., & Noam, G. (2012). *Evidence-based bullying prevention programs for children and youth.* San Francisco, CA: Jossey-Bass.

Sugai, G., Horner, R., & Algozzine, B. (2010). Reducing the effectiveness of bullying behavior in schools. Retrieved from http://www.pbis.org/common/cms/files/pbisresources/PBIS_Bullying_Behavior_Apr19_2011.pdf

Swearer, S. (2010). Bullying: What parents, teachers can do to stop it. American Psychological Association. Retrieved from http://www.apa.org/news/press/releases/2010/04/bullying.aspx

Swearer, S., Doces, M., Jones, L., & Collier, A. (2012). Bullying prevention 101 for schools: Dos and don'ts. Berkman Center Research Publication. No. 2013-2. Retrieved from http://dx.doi.org/10,2139/ssrn.2197951

Swearer, S., Espelage, D., & Napolitano, S. (2009). *Bullying prevention and intervention: Realistic strategies for schools.* New York, NY: Guilford Press.

Swearer, S., Wang, C., Magg, J., Siebecker, A., & Frerichs, L. (2012). Understanding the bullying dynamic among students in special and general education. *Journal of School Psychology, 50*, 503–520.

Sylvester, R. (2011). Teacher as bully: Knowingly or unintentionally harming students. *The Delta Gamma Bulletin, 77*(2), 42–46

Syversten, A., Flanagan, C., & Stout, M. (2009). Code of silence: Students' perceptions of school climate and willingness to intervene in a peer's dangerous plan. *Journal of Educational Psychology, 101*, 219–232.

Thapa, A., Cohen, J., Guffey, S., & Higgins-D'Alessandro, A. (2013). A review of school climate research. American Educational Research Association. Retrieved from http://www.ijvs.org/files/Publications/A%20Review%20of%20School%20Climate%20Research.pdf

Unnever, J., & Cornell, D. (2003). Bullying, self-control, and ADHD. *Journal of Interpersonal Violence, 18*, 129147.

U.S. Department of Education. (2010). Anti-bullying policies: Examples of provisions in state laws. Retrieved from http://www2.ed.gov/about/offices/list/opepd/ppss/reports.html#safe

U.S. Department of Education. (2011). Analysis of state bullying laws and policies. Retrieved from https://www2.ed.gov/rschstat/eval/bullying/state-bullying-laws/state-bullying-laws.pdf

U.S. Department of Education. (2013). Bullying, harassment, and civil rights: An overview of school districts' federal obligation to respond to harassment. Retrieved from http://www.stopbullying.gov/videos/2014/02/civil-rights.html

U.S. Department of Education. (2014). Guiding principles: A resource guide for improving school climate and discipline. Retrieved from http://www2.ed.gov/policy/gen/guid/school-discipline/guiding-principles.pdf

U.S. Department of Education. (n.d.). Bullying and children and youth with disabilities and special health needs. Retrieved from http://www.stopbullying.gov/at-risk/groups/special-needs/bullyingtipsheet.pdf

U.S. Department of Education, Office of Civil Rights. (2000). Dear colleague letter: Reminder of responsibility under Section 504 of the rehabilitative act. Retrieved from http://www2.ed.gov/about/offices/list/ocr/docs/disabharassltr.html

U.S. Department of Education, Office of Civil Rights. (2010). Dear colleague letter: Harassment and bullying. Retrieved from http://www2.ed.gov/about/offices/list/ocr/docs/dcl-factsheet-201010.pdf

U.S. Department of Education, Office of Civil Rights. (2014). Dear colleague letter: Responding to bullying of students with disabilities. Retrieved from http://www2.ed.gov/about/offices/list/ocr/letters/colleague-bullying-201410.pdf

U.S. Department of Education, Office of Special Education and Rehabilitative Services. (2013). Dear colleague letter and enclosure: Bullying of students with disabilities. Retrieved from https://www2.ed.gov/policy/speced/guid/idea/memosdcltrs/bullyingdcl-8-20-13.pdf

U.S. Department of Education & U.S. Department of Justice. (2014). Dear colleague letter: Non-discriminatory administration of school discipline. Retrieved from http://www.justice.gov/crt/about/edu/documents/dcl.pdf

U.S. Department of Health and Human Services, Substance Abuse and Mental Health Services Administration (SAMHSA). (2014a). Concept of trauma and guidance for a trauma informed approach. SAMHSA's Trauma and Justice Strategic Initiative. Retrieved from http://store.samhsa.gov/product/SAMHSA-s-Concept-of-Trauma-and-Guidance-for-a-Trauma-Informed-Approach/SMA14-4884

U.S. Department of Health and Human Services, Substance Abuse and Mental Health Services Administration (SAMHSA). (2014b). Treatment improvement protocol 57: Trauma-informed care in behavioral health services. Retrieved from http://store.samhsa.gov/product/TIP-57-Trauma-Informed-Care-in-Behavioral-Health-Services/SMA14-4816

Vaillancourt, T., Hymel, S., & McDougall, P. (2013). The biological underpinning of peer victimization: Understanding why and how the effects of bullying can last a lifetime. *Theory into Practice, 52*(4), 241–248. doi:10.1080/00405841.2013.82976

Walker, H., Horner, R., Sugai, G., Bullis, M., Sprague, J., Bricker, D., & Kaufman, M. (1996). Integrated approaches to preventing antisocial behavior patterns among school-age children and youth. *Journal of Emotional and Behavioral Disorders, 4*(4), 194–209.

Wang, W., Vaillancourt, T., Brittain, H., McDougall, P., Krygsman, A., Smith, D., . . . Hymel, S. (2014). School climate, peer victimization and academic achievement: Results from a multi-informant study. *School Psychology Quarterly, 29*(3), 360–377.

Washington State Office of the Education Ombudsman. (2011). Model procedure: Prohibition of harassment, intimidation, and bullying. Retrieved from http://www.digitalarchives.wa.gov/GovernorGregoire/oeo/reports/anti-bullying_model_procedure.pdf

Weissberg, R. (2013). Social and emotional learning: From research to national perspectives. Retrieved from http://safesupportivelearning.ed.gov/sites/default/files/SEL%20Webinar.pdf

Weissbound, R., Jones, S., Ross, T., Kahn, J., & Russell, M. (2014). *The children we mean to raise: The real messages adults are sending about values.* Cambridge, MA: Harvard Graduate School of Education. Retrieved from http://sites.gse.harvard.edu/sites/default/files/making-caring-common/files/mcc_report_the_children_we_mean_to_raise_0.pdf

Welcoming Schools. (n.d.). Welcoming schools: An inclusive approach to addressing family diversity, gender stereotyping and name calling in K-5 learning environments. Human Rights Council. Retrieved from http://www.welcomingschools.org/pages/download-an-introduction-to-welcoming-schools

Wright, J. (2003). Preventing classroom bullying: What teachers can do. Retrieved from http://www.jimwrightonline.com/pdfdocs/bully/bullyBooklet.pdf

Young, J., Ne'eman, A., & Gelser, S. (2011). Bullying and students with disabilities. Briefing paper. National Council on Disability. Retrieved from http://www.ncd.gov/publications/2011/March92011

Appendix

Planning Matrix

Core Components for Preventing and Responding to Bullying and Disability-Based Harassment

Rating

1: Exploration of research- and evidence-based programs
2: Beginning program development, identifying resources, and core components
3: Initial phase of implementation, staff training, and student activities
4: Full operation of program, ongoing multitiered interventions, and staff buy-in
5: Sustained practice and measured long-term outcomes

Core component	Objectives and criteria	Rating	Planned action/ target date for completion	Responsible individual(s)/ department
1. Multitiered interventions	a. District-level policies and procedures to define bullying and harassment	1 2 3 4 5		
	b. Classroom-level interventions (e.g., anti-bullying activities)			
	c. Individualized interventions for the bully, victim, and bystanders			

(continued)

Core component	Objectives and criteria	Rating	Planned action/ target date for completion	Responsible individual(s)/ department
2. Assessment	a. Monitoring and tracking bullying and harassment	1 2 3 4 5		
	b. Data-based decision making			
	c. Standard operating reporting procedures for students and staff			
	d. Survey of students on positive school climate and bullying			
	e. Transparency and accountability of bullying and harassment data and end-of-year reports			
3. Positive school climate	a. School leadership with a focus on respect and connectedness	1 2 3 4 5		
	b. Student leadership in all levels of decision making, engaged in anti-bullying activities			
	c. Safe learning environment with high expectations for all students			
	d. Equitable treatment for all staff and students			
4. Social-emotional learning	a. Adopted social-emotional learning (SEL) curriculum	1 2 3 4 5		
	b. Structured SEL lesson plans in all grade levels			
	c. Focus on self-awareness, interpersonal skills, and responsible decision making			

Core component	Objectives and criteria	Rating	Planned action/target date for completion	Responsible individual(s)/department
5. Skills-based learning	a. Teach appropriate skills with clear behavioral expectations	1 2 3 4 5		
	b. Bystander education programs in all grades			
	c. Graduated consequences and support services for students who bully			
	d. Targeted interventions for students with disabilities on how to respond to bullying			
	e. Explicit instruction on how to report bullying			
6. Staff training	a. Ongoing professional development for all staff on federal and state regulations	1 2 3 4 5		
	b. Training on the warning signs of bullying and long-term effects			
	c. Standard operating response protocol			
	d. Reporting requirements and review of disaggregated data by school and grade level			
7. Parent and community involvement	a. Involve parents and community stakeholders in the school safety team (SST)	1 2 3 4 5		
	b. Foster communication in a variety of formats			
	c. Recruit volunteers to participate in anti-bullying activities			
	d. Parent notification of a bullying incident			

(continued)

Core component	Objectives and criteria	Rating	Planned action/ target date for completion	Responsible individual(s)/ department
8. Supervise hot spots	a. Identify hot spots in the school and surrounding areas	1 2 3 4 5		
	b. Assign staff to supervise hot spots			
	c. Monitor adult supervision and review reporting data			
9. Ongoing sustained programs	a. Yearly quantitative and qualitative data reported to parents, students, and community	1 2 3 4 5		
	b. SST meet regularly with agenda and action steps			
	c. Leadership that articulates a clear shared vision with measurable goals			
	d. Leadership that holds teachers accountable for implementation and maintenance of core components			

Appendix

B

Additional Classroom Management Interventions

1. Examine and break down instructions to ensure they are clear and concrete as teachers can talk too much from time to time. Clear and concise instructions are the cornerstone for a positive classroom environment. Teachers who embed instructions in extraneous information and give long dialogues of instructions can expect students to become confused and exhibit inattention and off-task behaviors. Be prepared to break the task or lesson down into smaller parts during a task analysis. Teachers may incorrectly assume a student has mastered a prerequisite skill or thoroughly understands the directions, yet the student is struggling to stay on task or complete the assignment because he or she does not understand the beginning steps. Know each step for the intended lesson or task, and be prepared to break the skill into smaller steps if necessary to accommodate a student by switching to an introductory level or simpler task. It is important for teachers to move seamlessly within the lesson plan to maintain student behavior.

2. Provide students with a variety of effective prompts. Prompts are utilized to assist the student in mastering a new skill or maintaining appropriate behaviors. One type of prompt is modeling the appropriate response for students. For example, the teacher models the steps for turning in homework to the proper file on the front bookshelf in addition to the verbal instructions. Another prompt is teacher proximity to the student. Proximity control has been used as an effective prompt by teachers to maintain positive behaviors and student engagement. Teachers should sit or stand closer to students who are exhibiting mild behavior intrusions (e.g., turning around in their seats or fidgeting with materials). This technique should not be used as an act of authority if the behavior is more severe or has escalated to the point of crisis, as the teacher should remain

Recognize, Respond, Report: Preventing and Addressing Bullying of Students with Special Needs
by Lori Ernsperger. Copyright © 2016 by Paul H. Brookes Publishing Co., Inc.

a safe distance from the student without direct body confrontation. Another type of prompts includes visual supports to identify classroom expectations. Visual signs for "sit quietly," "hands to self," and "eyes on the teacher" can greatly increase student engagement and compliance. Written checklists are a helpful visual tool for students to review the required steps for completing an assignment. Teachers can also utilize gestural prompts when teaching students new skills as well as to remind students of class rules for maintaining appropriate behaviors. Caution is taken if the teacher is relying solely on verbal reprimands, verbal reminders, or verbal prompts to redirect a student's behavior.

3. Respect all students equally. It can be very demeaning to a student if a teacher states, "He is just too lazy to finish his work," or "She does not *want* to participate in class." Applying subjective statements to students with disabilities is inaccurate and denies the student important educational supports based on anecdotal opinions. If a student is displaying low-level interfering behaviors, talk to the student directly and discreetly to determine the cause. For example, a student who is off-task with her head on a desk may have experienced harmful bullying during the passing period. Teachers should seek to understand the root cause of the student's misbehavior. To the extent possible, de-escalate with empathy and provide clear instructions with prompts for the initial steps of the required task. Avoid comments or directions from across the room that are general in nature (e.g., "You kids need to get to work"). Instead, approach the student and with a neutral tone of voice state the instruction, "Open your book to page 52." Provide assistance as the student begins the task, and quickly reinforce for on-task, compliant behaviors.

4. Provide self-management tools. Student self-management tools are an effective system for monitoring student behavior. Research suggests that self-management techniques teach students appropriate independent skills and help reduce interfering behaviors where students monitor and provide feedback on their behavior. The steps for self-management include first identifying a behavior or goal for reduction or to increase (e.g., reduce blurting out in class and increase raising hand to request assistance). The teacher may need to demonstrate the appropriate behavior and role-play with the student to practice. Second, select a recording system and teach the student how to document their behavior (e.g., one tally mark for each time raising hand to request assistance or, for a younger child, one sad face for getting up without permission). Third, the most important step for implementing a self-management system is identifying goals, reinforcers, and determining the criteria for receiving reinforcement: How many tally marks does a student need to earn 15 extra minutes on the computer? How many smiley faces does the student need to take a break on the computer? The teacher and student should monitor and evaluate overall success in order for the student to self-evaluate. This type of individualized intervention can be implemented for a short period to teach new skills (e.g., raising hand to request assistance for a 2-week period). The program should be altered or faded based on data analysis and student outcomes.

5. Write a contract with the student and consider individualizing the reinforcement schedule or the frequency of reinforcement. A student contract includes the criteria for earning reinforcement or a reinforcement schedule. A contract is clearly written with criteria for student success, and it identifies reinforcement for the student. As mentioned, reinforcers do not have to be costly or time-consuming. Students may select from a potential list of reinforcers such as reading the school announcements, eating lunch with the principal, listening to music during free time, selecting a game for the entire class, or selecting a tangible item from the treasure chest.

Appendix

Sample Dear Abby Letters

Please read the following "Dear Abby" letters from students. Put yourself in their shoes. What does it feel like to be bullied in school? What advice can you give that might make a difference? Have you ever experienced a similar situation? If so, please share.

Dear Friend,

My school allows bullying. We have a lot of students who fight and it can be a scary place. I have one teacher who is always yelling at me. I try my best, but I am just not good at math. I get anxious about coming to school and tell my mom I have a headache. My friends and I want to start an anti-bullying group, but we don't want the teachers to get mad. I am scared to tell other teachers because I am not sure they will believe me. What do I do about my math teacher?

Tiffani, MO

Dear Friend,

I am bullied at school every day for the music I listen to and the clothes I wear. If I do anything different, this group of baseball players won't leave me alone. I have tried to talk to a few teachers, and they say not to worry about it but that doesn't work. I ignore them and try not to let it bother me, but when I get home I am so angry with everyone and everything. It is super frustrating. What can I do about this group of bullies?

Autumn, KY

Dear Friend,

I have ADD and have to take medication at school. The teachers are not helping and make me sit in the back of the classroom. Some of the kids call me horrible names, and I am often tortured on the bus. The bus driver is worthless. I try to make everybody happy, but I am super sad. How can I stop the nightmare on the bus? I really don't know what to say when they call me retarded.

Cory, SC

Dear Friend,

I am not bullied at school, but my friend is bullied. She is tall, has pimples, and is kind of a nerd. We have been friends since kindergarten, but now I am not sure what to do. She is never invited to any parties. I have seen her get pushed around and called names. I don't want to say anything to the bullies because I don't want to be their next target. Sometimes I just laugh along with them and tell my friend it's a joke. I feel so guilty about not doing anything. What can I do?

Allie, MI

Dear Friend,

I moved to Florida when I was 8 years old. I was picked on, yelled at, and even punched by other students. They mostly call me "gay" and "fag," but I am not homosexual. It is the same group of boys. I want to be homeschooled, but my mom said "no." I don't want to tell any of the teachers because I am sure this will make it worse. I still feel like the new kid, and I don't have any real friends. How do I defend myself without punching them in the face?

Adam, FL

Dear Friend,

I am a straight-A, honor-roll student and I just won the school's "most improved" award, but I am still bullied by several girls in my class. I used to be overweight, but I lost the weight and look much better. These girls will not let it go or leave me alone. The school counselor told me to ignore them and she changed my schedule to different classes, but it is not any better. I would like to be friends with these girls, but I am confused. Any help would be appreciated.

Melanie, NV

Dear Friend,

I can't believe this is happening to me. I am a good student and have some close friends, but I just found out that another group of girls created a fake Facebook page with my picture. They post cruel comments and spread rumors about me and guys. I haven't done anything to them. If I tell my parents, they will just take away my phone and laptop. Yesterday they posted a picture of a naked girl and called me a slut. I have to do something quickly. This is out of control.

Fergal, Ireland

Appendix

D

Sample Social Narrative

The CALM Approach to Bullying at School

Sometimes at school, other kids will try to bully me. This can happen to anyone. The CALM approach (developed by Dr. Michelle Borba) challenges us to cool down, assert ourselves, look bullies in the eye, and mean it.

I need to remember to be CALM. Cool down and take a breath.

Stand up tall.

Look them in the eye.

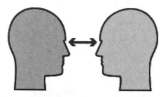

Mean it and tell them, "Leave me alone."

I also need to tell the teacher.

I can make it better.

Appendix

Example Bullying and Harassment Report

According to school district policy, bullying and harassment is unwanted, aggressive behavior among school-age children that involves a real or perceived power imbalance. The behavior is repeated or has the potential to be repeated over time. Bullying includes actions such as making threats, spreading rumors, cyberbullying, attacking someone physically or verbally, and excluding someone from a group on purpose. All reports of bullying will be investigated.

Today's date: _____ School: _____

Name of person reporting incident: _____ Grade: _____

Type of report (circle one):   Self-report   Peer report   Staff report

                                 Parent report   Anonymous report

Name of student (victim): _____ Age: _____ Grade: _____

Did the incident involve a protected class?
(race/national origin/religion/gender/sexual preference/disability)?   Yes   No

If yes, please list:

Date and approximate time of incident: _____

Location of incident (circle all that apply):

Hallway   Restroom   Classroom   Gym   Lunchroom

Playground   Bus   Before/after school   School-sponsored event   Electronic means (cyberbullying)

Name(s) of alleged offenders (including adults or staff):

_____ Age: _____ School: _____

_____ Age: _____ School: _____

_____ Age: _____ School: _____

_____ Age: _____ School: _____

Type of bullying or harassment (circle all that apply):

Physical bullying (hitting, kicking, shoving)   Threatening

Social exclusion or rejection   Taunting/name-calling/insulting

Cyberbullying/electronic communication   Spreading harmful rumors

Damaging property   Intimidation

Did anyone else witness the bullying, including any adult or staff?   Yes   No

If yes, please list:

Please describe the incident or any further comments:

_____

For Administrative Use Only
Official designee signature:
Date received: Assigned case #:

_____

Appendix

Bullying and Harassment Auditing Checklist

	Yes/No	Comments
1. Can you define bullying and disability-based harassment (or harassment of other protected classes) and identify federal regulations for protecting students with disabilities?		
2. Does the school have a school safety team (SST) with parents, students, and community stakeholders? Does the SST meet regularly to coordinate schoolwide activities and disseminate best practice guidelines for preventing bullying?		
3. Has the school developed and disseminated a universal reporting form for all staff, students, and others to report incidents of bullying (paper and/or online)? Are all staff required to report bullying?		

(continued)

	Yes/No	Comments
4. Is a school official designee responsible for collecting and investigating reports of bullying? Are parents notified if their child is involved in an incident of bullying (within one school day)?		
5. Is professional development provided to all staff members each school year to help prevent and encourage the proper response to bullying and harassment? Has the school adopted a standard operating protocol for all adults when responding to a bullying incident (e.g., Stop-Talk-Walk)?		
6. Does the school provide bystander education on what to do during a bullying incident and how to safely intervene and report to an adult? Does the school district provide ongoing age-appropriate instruction to students on bullying prevention and social-emotional learning (SEL) skills?		
7. Does the school regularly survey students about whether they feel safe, respected, and cared about in school? Does the survey ask specific questions regarding rates of bullying? Are survey results posted on the district's web site?		
8. Does the school have a written plan that includes policies, procedures, and measurable outcomes and interventions to address bullying (e.g., a technical assistance guide)?		
9. Does the school district annually assess, review, and report the number and nature of incidents of reported bullying and harassment?		

Index

Tables and figures are indicated by *t* and *f*, respectively.